THE GOLDEN YEARS

Chronicles and Challenges of "Being Old"

"They also serve who only stand and wait."
John Milton, Sonnet XVI

THE GOLDEN YEARS

Chronicles and Challenges of "Being Old"

Paul J. Lavin, Ph.D.
Brian Kelly, Editor

Rafka Press
Phoenix, Arizona

Copyright © 2020 Paul Lavin, Ph.D.

Typesetting, layout, cover design, copyright © 2020 Rafka Press LLC.

All rights reserved. No part of this book may be reproduced or transmitted in any form or by any means, electronic or mechanical, including photocopying, recording, or by any information storage or retrieval system now existing or to be invented, without written permission from the respective copyright holder(s), except for the inclusion of brief quotations in a review.

The Scripture citations used in this work are taken from the *Saint Joseph New Catholic Edition of the HOLY BIBLE*, Copyright © 1962 by Catholic Book Publishing Company, NY.

Published by
Rafka Press LLC
Phoenix, Arizona, USA

ISBN-13: 978-0-9911958-3-1

Library of Congress Control Number: 2020943328

10 9 8 7 6 5 4 3 2 1

Visit us online at www.rafkapress.com
For more information: info@rafkapress.com

Contents

Preface vii

Introduction 1

The use of time: The foundation on which our
salvation is built. 9

They ("Being Old" pain sufferers) also serve who
only stand and wait
Part 1. 17

They ("Being Old" pain sufferers) also serve who
only stand and wait
Part 2. 31

They ("Being Old" pain sufferers) also serve who
only stand and wait
Part 3. 43

Reflections on exaltation of the Holy Cross 47

A plea to "Being Old" sufferers from the souls
in Purgatory 55

Reflections on seemingly unanswered prayers. . . 61

"Being Old" reflections on "the way we were" . . 71

Warning to "Being Old" sufferers: Take the
devil seriously 83

Be prepared: Thinking as Our Lord intended
will be challenging 97

Reinstating the Holy Rosary and devotions to
   Our Blessed Mother 103

A spiritual war of words 115

Epilogue 133

Preface

This book is about being old. The "Being Old" stage, as I call it, is the final stage of life. It is markedly different from all the stages, which precede it. The "Being Old" stage ends with death. Infancy, childhood, adolescence, adulthood, and middle age are the normal stages that we all pass through, barring no ill-health, accidents, or catastrophic events, leading us to an earlier than expected demise. Prior to arriving at the "Being Old" stage, thoughts about death and coping with the infirmities associated with it are few and far between. Our main focus is on occupational advancement, paying bills, rearing a family, socializing with friends, and socking away some money for the future.

Most of us make arrangement for some form of retirement and plan ahead accordingly. Caring for grandchildren, visiting and traveling with friends, attending sporting and cultural events, and doing volunteer work at a community center might be activities that we look forward to. We have been told that these are the "golden years," our time to enjoy the fruits of our labor, which we are entitled to after working for the past thirty or more years. We enter retirement believing that the best years are just over the horizon. The old saying, "You are as young as you feel," applies to you—and right now you feel great.

For me, the myth surrounding the "golden years" was shattered when a colleague of mine retired after completing thirty-five years of service as a university professor. He was honored by the university and left his post while he was "at the top of his game." He was healthy, mentally sharp, and energetic, looking forward to the years ahead. Consulting opportunities were made available if he wanted to make some extra money; his marriage of forty years was a happy one; his children were married and living close by; and he was a proud grandfather. My friend had much to look forward to.

Within two years, all of this changed. My friend was diagnosed with terminal cancer and had only a short time left to live. He lost a considerable amount of weight and appeared emaciated. This intelligent, energetic, and socially vibrant man was struggling from day to day, making every effort to gracefully cope with his malignant affliction. In one of my last conversations with him, I specifically recall him saying, "The golden years aren't so golden." Although my friend died three decades ago, I never forgot his assessment of the "golden years" and the false promises that these two words convey.

Now that I have entered the golden years, I have a much better understanding of what really happens to us as we pass through the last stage of life. "Being Old" leads us into loss—the gradual and sometimes quick loss of those human powers that we once so easily performed and had learned to take for granted.

Losing your powers is a lonely journey—a venture that begins and ends on a road paved with suffering. This suffering is not only physical but emotional and spiritual as well.

The devil will be working extra hard during your golden years. He will fill your mind with doubt—especially doubt about Our Lord's promises, the efficacy of suffering, and the importance of suffering in redeeming our sins and those of the people we love. He will try to get you to despair, hoping that like Judas, you will take your life and lose your soul. The devil will also tempt you using envy and anger, two of his favorite Capital Sins. He will prepare a "custom-made plan" like a suit, which is specifically designed to fit you, a "Being Old" sufferer who only has a short time left to live on this planet. You can count on the devil to throw extra coal on the fire in his last-ditch attempts to lure you away from Our Lord and into his clutches.

This book is not only about being old. It is also about suffering—the suffering of old folks whose pain is chronic and ubiquitous—pain which seems to come out of nowhere when least expected. It focuses on how the offering of one's pain can serve as "payback" for one's sins and the sins of deceased loved ones who may be languishing in the fire of Purgatory. Because we live in presumptuous times, the souls in Purgatory are ignored. How many of these poor souls might be screaming out right now, pleading for our help? We, who are alive, can still earn merit, which could be applied to lessening their sentence in this fire-filled exile. Picture your grandparents,

parents, uncles, aunts, and friends being tossed about in a sea of fire. When Our Lady appeared to the three children at Fatima in 1917, she showed them a vision of Hell. The vision was so frightening it was terminated after a few seconds. Many saints who have been shown Purgatory describe it as a temporary hell. However, these souls suffer with great joy, content to be purged by the will of God, and in the certain knowledge that they are saved and will see God in Heaven. Who among us "Being Old" sufferers would deny those whom we loved on earth our prayers and offerings, which could alleviate their suffering? Yet, this is what is happening today. The good news is that we still have the gift of life. Hence, we can continue to earn merit for ourselves and those whom we once loved on earth but may have now forgotten.

The central theme of this book focuses upon the expiatory value of suffering. My professional and personal thoughts concerning prayers, devotions, and reflections on the Catholic Church and the changes that have occurred over the past fifty years are included. I have attempted to put words on these experiences, describing how the changes have affected me and those of my generation. Hopefully you, the reader, will find this book to be of value in better understanding "Being Old" and how we can best serve Our Lord by gracefully carrying the crosses assigned to us in this final and most challenging stage of life on earth.

Introduction

There is an old saying that has become popular for those of us now living in the final stage of life—"Growing old is not for sissies." While this mantra has some truth attached to it, it is the word "growing" with which I would take issue. For me, it is "being old," not growing old that is most challenging.

Growing old begins once we have left our mother's womb. It is at this time that the process of aging begins. As we pass through childhood, adolescence, adulthood, and middle age, our differing potentials begin to actualize and mature. This actualization enables us to better cope with and improve the quality of our life. Barring what the world would label as "misfortune" or a string of "bad luck," most of us become intellectually sharper, more socially skilled, and occupationally savvy with the passage of time and the normal acquisition of worldly experience. When we become truly old this changes. Doing better ceases and deterioration sets in until body and soul must separate.

Some examples of the preceding are as follows. Simple fine-motor skills that you could once perform "automatically" become increasingly more difficult. Buttoning your clothes is one such example. Coordinating your thumbs and forefingers so that the buttons slide into the slits of your clothing becomes stressful. The buttons keep slipping out of your fingers. Like a spoiled child, they refuse to cooperate. "How could such an activity, which was once so easy, become so frustrating?" you ask yourself. "My hands just don't work right anymore," you lament.

Tasks requiring fine-motor skills are not the only movements that become frustrating. Activities requiring balance, bending, squatting, and stretching become problematic as well. For instance, if you drop an item onto the floor, you might hesitate before bending down to pick it up. "Is it worth the effort or should I leave it there?" you ask yourself. It wasn't that long ago, when you could have performed this task with the snap of your fingers. Now you feel like the Tin Man from the *Wizard of Oz*, creaking and groaning—waiting for your joints to become lubricated so that you can perform the ordinary activities of everyday living. Again, this doesn't get better with the passage of time and effort. Exercise might help to slow the deterioration, but muscular flexibility, a gift of youth, eventually becomes a victim of being old.

"And what about my memory?" you ask. Finding the words to express your thoughts may become increasingly more frustrating. You might find your mind blocked in trying to recall names, events, and facts that once rolled off your tongue with no effort and at times were expressed eloquently. What is now called a "senior moment" occurs with greater frequency. You might also notice that concentrating has become a problem. You seem to drift in and out of consciousness. You find yourself steering off into space with a far-away look in your eyes—oblivious to what is going on around you. Again, making a concerted effort to stay active and involved with your surroundings will help you to slow any deterioration. Despite our best efforts, however, deterioration is inevitable.

The preceding are just a few of the changes that old folks, who are in the final years of life, encounter. When you become old, the powers, which you once took for granted, gradually or even quickly erode. Sicknesses don't necessarily get better; wounds don't heal as expected; and aches, pains, and diseases seem to be forever ongoing. If one malady finally abates, another soon arises to replace it. Holding your own—not losing ground—is considered a victory.

Observing the decline and eventual loss of your powers can be anxiety evoking to say the least. Who among us doesn't find this to be frightening? And who among us wants others to see us struggling, straining, and fighting to maintain our ground in our battle with natural decline. This final stage of life, which I call "Being Old," begins at about age sixty-five and lasts until we die. Our health, financial resources, and social support are determining factors as to whether "Being Old" goes on for a few years or several decades thereafter.

As a psychologist—a "Being Old" Catholic psychologist at that—I have attempted to combine my professional field of study with my Faith to better understand and cope with "Being Old" challenges. About five years ago, I was diagnosed with Parkinson's disease. This in combination with a number of other health-related issues has led to chronic pain, which at times can be intense and unrelenting. Chronic pain, unlike any other of life's experiences, is most humbling. Chronic pain can become so agonizing that it demands our full concentration, often trumping even our most noble efforts to cope with it gracefully. Attempts to pray, seeking God's help, can be lost in these agonizing moments. Reciting those prayers, which we had committed to memory since childhood, is arduous. Again, pain can and often does trump our best efforts to emulate Our Lord and the great saints of the Catholic Church in these trying times. This is what makes coping with pain so humbling.

"Being Old" is the central theme appearing throughout this book. It is written for those suffering Catholics in the senescent stage of life—those whose chronic pain seriously impedes or keeps them from participating in those activities, which fill the lives of the healthy old folks who have not yet been forced to the sidelines. Despite the ages of the latter, they can still travel, play tennis, golf, drive an automobile, and perform those activities enabling them to function independently. These folks may be chronologically old, but they are "still in the game" we might say. Their lives are in marked contrast to those old, chronic pain sufferers whose powers are slipping away despite their best efforts.

A word of caution is worthy of note here. "Old Scratch," the name of the devil in Stephen Vincent Benet's book entitled *The Devil and Daniel Webster,* will use his most diabolical ploys to arouse feelings of envy and anger within those of us who are fast losing our powers. If you are one of the unhealthy old folks, Old Scratch will repeatedly whisper the following into your ear: "Why should they (the healthy aged) have it so good, while you, a devoted Catholic, are suffering and are unable to enjoy even the simplest of life's pleasures?" "After all, aren't these supposed to be the golden years?" "What a rip off! Where is your God when you need Him?" Keep in mind that Old Scratch will use questions such as the preceding to trick you into underrating the importance of suffering and its satisfactory value in saving your soul and the souls of your loved ones. He knows full well that envy and anger are Capital Sins that can lure us into damnation.

In reading the lives of the saints, their ability to embrace suffering strikes me as amazingly courageous. As indicated previously, coping with chronic pain is a humbling experience. When caught in the midst of my agony, I sometimes feel like a man holding on to the edge of a cliff, whose knuckles have turned white, straining to keep myself from falling into a dark abyss. Unlike the great saints, I hardly am able to embrace my suffering and would prefer avoiding it altogether. When my flesh is screaming for relief, Old Scratch turns up the heat, tempting me to "throw in the towel" so to speak—to despair. "Yes" fellow Catholics! It is despair—the loss of faith and purpose that Old Scratch uses in his attempts to trap me. The challenge for me is to keep hope in the forefront of my mind while praying during these trying moments.

When reflecting on the impact of despair and its effect on those of us in the "Being Old" stage, the work of Erik Erikson, a well-known developmental psychologist, comes to mind. According to Erikson, a psychosocial conflict between ego integrity and despair confronts us in the final stage of life. By successfully resolving this conflict, we acquire the virtue of wisdom. This in turn enables us to look back upon our lives with a sense of accomplishment. Feelings of contentment and approaching death without fear will follow. On the other hand, those who view their past as consisting of unfulfilled goals and guilt, end their lives on a hopeless, despairing note. Regretting that their time on earth is ending and lamenting that there is no second chance dominates much of their thinking. Like most secular psychologists, Erikson fails to take God into account. He leaves us with no specifics on how we can earn merit through our suffering right up to the moment of death. Rather, we are left with our own devices, while Old Scratch assails us with dark thoughts; suffering is of no value and is being inflicted upon us by an uncaring and merciless God.

Although I have been a practicing psychologist for more than forty years, I have found little solace in reading the works of those secular psychologists who have written about death and dying. Focusing on past accomplishments, earthly honors and glory, and relationships with family and friends are not particularly helpful when intense pain begins to carry out a full-scale attack aimed at all facets of my physical anatomy. It is at these times that I thank God for sending His Son to suffer for the remediation of our sins. By suffering on the cross, Our Lord fulfilled the purpose of His life and set an example for us to follow. We, too, can offer our suffering as a prayer for the remediation of our sins and those of our loved ones. When all else is taken away, such an offering can provide us with the strength to endure—a purpose for living in a world that views suffering as a curse rather than a blessing. It is my fellow "Being Old" chronic pain sufferers to whom I dedicate the forthcoming pages of this book. Hopefully the reading of these will help to make your lives more meaningful and give greater purpose to your remaining time on earth.

The use of time:
The foundation on which
our salvation is built

Time is one of the most important gifts given to us by Our Lord. The use of time, in the way that Our Lord intended, will lead to eternal happiness with Him in Heaven. This, He promised to us on numerous occasions. Squandering this precious gift, however, could lead to the everlasting damnation of our immortal soul. Throughout Holy Scripture, Our Lord promised this as well.

The first of January, the Feast of the Circumcision of Our Lord, begins each calendar year. This great feast celebrates the day on which Jesus first shed His blood for our sins. This celebration is also referred to as the Octave Day of Christmas on the Church's calendar.

Each upcoming New Year, we are told, presents us with the opportunity to begin anew — a chance to start over and catch the happiness, which has alluded us in the past. So, in the spirit of the day, we, like other "Being Old" cohorts of our generation, might make light-hearted promises to do better — *resolutions* we call them. The promises we make at the beginning of the New Year are a fun-filled way to pass our time and share jokes with friends about our shortcomings. We pretend to commit ourselves to overcoming some minor character flaw or bad habit. However, shortly thereafter, the resolution gets broken. But who takes making resolutions seriously? Resolutions, we rationalize, are made to be broken. Deep down we know that with the passing of time nothing will change. Every New Year begins with "the same old, same old" rituals and ends in stagnation. Making resolutions is simply a way to pass time until the next New Year's Eve party, after 365 days have dropped from the calendar.

As we pass through middle age into the "Being Old" stage of life, we become increasingly more aware in recognizing the preceding for what it is—a silly waste of time. We recognize that the gift of time does not last forever. Time, like everything else in this world, runs out. How we have used our "time gone by" then becomes critical. Whether our soul is saved or damned will depend on this. Salvation or damnation will be the only alternatives. There will be no place in between—no second chance so that we can try again. Thinking about this, of course, can be a frightening prospect, particularly if we have failed to prepare ourselves for the inevitable. Avoidance is so much easier in the short run.

The world's perception on the passing of time and how it should be used differs markedly from that which Our Lord teaches us. The lyrics of popular songs are good examples of the former. For instance, the song entitled "As Time Goes By" has become a classic in this regard. "As Time Goes By" was authored by Herman Hupfled in 1931. It was written for the musical *Everybody's Welcome*. While the song was well received, it reached its pinnacle of fame ten years later, a fame which continues to this day.

"As Time Goes By" became the signature song, which was sung by the piano player, Sam, in the movie *Casablanca*. *Casablanca* was released in 1942. This classic film starred Humphrey Bogart (Rick) and Ingrid Bergman (Ilsa). Most "Being Old" readers of my generation will recall that the movie took place at the beginning of World War II when Nazi Germany was the dominant force in North Africa. It was a time in which the best and worst characteristics of mankind unveiled themselves in the quest for power and monetary gain. Romance and the trials of forbidden love between Rick and Ilsa are the underlying themes throughout the movie. "As Time Goes By" is the love song unifying their relationship. It was their love song, the stiletto which opened old wounds unleashing great pain associated with their past.

While the melody is pleasant to the human ear, it is the lyrics which convey the writer's perception of time and those events that repeatedly occur with its passing. Note the lyrics at the song's beginning. So there are the simple facts of life, facts that are immutable, carved into stone. These cannot be changed and will always repeat themselves "As Time Goes By." The lyrics continue on, identifying these simple unchangeable facts.

These are the immutable truths, which are self-evident — truths that are "never out of date" and "no one can deny." Human love — love between a man and a woman. This is the driving, instinctual force that governs our behavior as we pass from one generation to the next. Unfortunately, these simple facts leave us with an empty palate when our time on earth runs out. What about Our Lord and Our Lady's promises? What about the love and graces that they promised to shower upon those of us who remained loyal and persevered up to the moment of our demise? These simple truths, which are "never out of date," are absent in "As Time Goes By." There will be no solace here unless we have prepared ourselves accordingly.

My rumination on "As Time Goes By"—one of the most popular songs ever written—came about while I was reading a sermon first delivered by Father Mary Benedict Hughes, CMRI, on January 1, 2012 (Sermon: "Circumcision," *The Four Marks*, January 2016, p. 4). Father Hughes's sermon focused on the upcoming New Year and how January 1 should serve as a reminder on the value of time and using God's gift of time wisely. His eloquent discourse on this most important topic was as follows:

> What a gift we have with the time that God has given to us! We don't know how many years we have left on earth before God calls us to render an account. Let us especially reflect upon, and value, the time that God gives us. How many people are there, who waste, who squander, the time that God gives them? How many people are there who are bored and again waste the time that they have? We

on the other hand should look upon it as a very precious gift because one day it will cease. Time will be no more.

We refer to the end of the world as the end of time. In fact, for each person who passes out of this world, at that moment, time for that person ceases. When we think about using time and the value of time, think this thought to yourself. How much would a soul of the damned in Hell give for one minute, even a few seconds of the time we so often squander? How much would they give for that few brief moments to be able to come back to the world and to make an act of perfect contrition, to go to confession, to repent and to regain the state of sanctifying grace? On the other hand, how much would the just in Heaven give for another minute of time to earn a higher place in Heaven, to gain greater merit? Think of that when you are tempted to waste time. Let us use the time God gives us to grow in grace, to sanctify ourselves, to practice virtue. There is a saying that time is worth God and that's quite a striking statement.

What that means is that in a moment of time a sinner, who is in a state of mortal sin, could gain God and sanctifying grace by an act of perfect contrition or devout confession. And likewise, one who is in a state of grace could lose God in just a moment of time. So time is precious. It is very valuable. It is something that we must use and be grateful for…So, let us thank God for the time, for the wonderful gift of time He has given to us. Let us make certain that we will use the time we have. Maybe next year on January 1st of 2017, there will be some of us present today, who will no longer be on this earth. We don't know. We don't know how much time God gives us. Let us use the time that we have and use it to earn a high place in Heaven.

Father Hughes's emphasis upon the significance of time struck a resounding note within me—maybe because I am in the final stage of life, and now realize that this precious commodity is fast running out. There is an end to the time allotted to us here on earth, and my useless squandering of this during my youthful and middle age years is now regretted. What a difference a few minutes can make! As Father Hughes so eloquently stated, it can make all the difference. A last-minute act of perfect contrition, which would take a short time, could lead to the salvation of one's immortal soul. The failure to do so could lead to one's damnation. I thought of "the good thief," Dismas, who petitioned Our Lord to take him into Heaven with Him, while they were suffering on the cross. Our Lord granted his petition. In less than a minute, this life-long reprobate's sins were forgiven, and he "stole" his way into paradise. Again, what a difference a few seconds can make. What wouldn't a condemned soul give for just a few minutes of extended time here on earth—a last-minute opportunity to avoid the pains of being punished for eternity?

Let me end this on a more positive note. Father Hughes points out that an extra few minutes of well-used time could also earn for us a higher place in Heaven. How often do we think about praying, sacrificing, and doing good works to earn greater happiness than that which would be allotted to us at the moment of death? Why be satisfied with just edging our way over the line when we could actually attain a higher degree of heavenly glory by wisely using a few minutes of time while we can still earn merit? Keep in mind that Our Lord promised us that the greater our prayers and good works, the greater would be our reward in Heaven. Consider Our Lord's words in Matthew 16:27: "For the Son of Man will come with his angels in his Father's glory and then he will repay everyone according to his conduct." Again, who among us would not wish for a few extra minutes of earthly time to make this possible? This is food for thought, especially those of us "Being Old" Catholics, who still have the gift of life and the potential to use this wisely "As Time Goes By." The wise use of time, as Our Lord intended, could turn the world's pyrite into heavenly gold and make the "golden years" on earth truly golden.

They ("Being Old" pain sufferers) also serve who only stand and wait
Part 1

As noted previously, there is a difference between growing old and being old. We all pass through life's stages, during which physical, social, and emotional changes, common to our species, occur. For example, infants begin life crawling from point A to point B. As they mature, they learn to stand, walk, and run from one place to the next. With the passage of time and exposure to ordinary worldly experiences, the infant "grows" and becomes an independent adult. An infant, who has now grown into adulthood, no longer has to rely on crawling to get from one place to another. He can drive an automobile, book passage on an airplane, or take other forms of transportation to locations where he wants to go. A young, middle-aged man or woman, with the passage of time and the acquisition of worldly skills, is now able to navigate the globe and conduct important business, leading to greater financial success.

As the years pass by, however, our ability to perform the preceding tasks diminishes and eventually ceases. Adjustment to "Being Old" begins to set in. Activities, which were once easily done, are taken away—never to return no matter what course of action is taken. Again, as noted previously, just "holding your own"—not losing any ground is a victory. It is at this point that gracefully coping with "Being Old" becomes the final and most important task in the remaining years of your life.

As stated previously, "Being Old" is challenging, especially when chronic pain enters into the picture. Make no mistake about it! There is a good chance that if you are in the "Being Old" stage, you will be assailed by chronic pain in one form or another. Remember Old Scratch. He will earnestly attempt to lead you into despair when given the slightest opportunity. And chronic pain is a major weapon in his arsenal.

In order to try and neutralize Old Scratch's attack, let's examine the dynamics of chronic pain, how it affects us, and what we can do to better cope with it. We might begin by comparing chronic pain to an obnoxious intruder who doesn't know when he is not wanted. The longer he stays, the more antagonistic he becomes. Even blatantly forthright requests asking him to leave are either ignored or overlooked. He is truly what we call "hard-headed," totally insensitive to the feelings of those persons around him.

Chronic pain has a number of names and causes. Sometimes it is called cancer, although numerous other physical and mental maladies can be at the root of the problem. Chronic pain can surround and penetrate your entire body. It saps your physical, emotional, and spiritual strength like a dry sponge that can never be saturated, no matter how much liquid is provided for its thirsty appetite. There are few respites from chronic pain. It is forever present, hounding us during the day and night.

Chronic pain can keep you internally focused—self-absorbed you might say. The sufferer can be constantly thinking about the state of his or her health. His thoughts can become dominated by the desire for even the slightest relief, a sign that the pain might abate and stop altogether. The sufferer yearns for the day that he can come back to the world and be involved in the events of everyday living. He hopes that he once again can become connected with healthy family and friends, who bring him warmth and encouragement, assuring him that he will get better.

But this might be the rub for the "Being Old" chronic pain sufferer. Deep down inside, he is fast losing confidence that his life will ever return to a normal state. He fears that more unremitting pain may be just over the horizon. "How many times can you get knocked down and get up off of the canvas?" he asks. The "pile on" of one repeated illness on top of the other may have become a consistent pattern. "Why should this change now or ever for that matter?" he laments. Doubt and anxiety plague him every step of the way. And then there is death, the Grim Reaper in a black robe, eagerly waiting to escort him to the final judgment. This is what he fears most. Yet nobody talks about this. It stays locked up within him, bursting at the seams, seeking at least one other person to whom he can express how he feels. All hope can become crushed when the "Being

Old" sufferer's psyche is caught in this whirlpool of mental and emotional anguish.

When one is in chronic pain, graciously interacting with others can be a major difficulty. They ask how you feel, and the sufferer's standard answer is "good," even though deep down he or she feels miserable. Pretending that the sufferer is in good spirits and acting as though he is interested in worldly endeavors is difficult when he feels isolated from the human race. But who wants to be viewed as a deadbeat (no pun intended) to those people who are trying to cheer him up? So the sufferer puts on a façade, making believe that he, too, is optimistic, although he really feels frightened, exhausted, and irritated with the course his life has taken. Smiling, asking and answering simple questions, and making small talk is harder than anyone can imagine, especially when his insides are screaming for relief and wishing that Christ would miraculously take this cross off of his shoulders.

In the sea of people surrounding him, what the sufferer longs for most is human compassion, true understanding, and genuine support in confronting this long and lonely battle. The search for these qualities in those around him can be a most difficult one. Healthy people say that they understand. They mean well and sincerely believe that this is so. But if you are a "Being Old" sufferer in a hospital or nursing home, when the visiting hours end, the visitors exit the premises. Many breathe a sigh of relief as they leave and go to their homes. It can be emotionally exhausting, watching a loved one suffer. It makes them aware of their own vulnerability, and they are momentarily thankful that God has not yet willed this upon them.

For those who leave, this ordeal is over, at least for now. They go home and continue to engage in the ordinary functional activities of life—activities which are easily performed—activities in which chronic pain doesn't interfere with every thought and movement of daily living. For the ordinary person, tying his shoes, brushing his teeth, toileting and bathing, and feeding himself are performed automatically. No forethought or planning is required. For the "Being Old" chronic pain sufferer, however, these simple tasks can be a major undertaking requiring help from a care-taker and the use of mechanical devices just so that you can put on your socks and shoes and tie them. Washing, drying, toileting, eating, and moving or hobbling from point A to point B are exhausting, especially if you are making the effort to do these independently—fighting to get better so that you can rejoin the human race.

This is chronic pain. It has a beginning but no predictable ending, always leaving the sufferer in an uncertain state. Chronic pain can rob you of your dignity. Even the strongest sufferer can fall into despair. For the "Being Old" sufferer, the days can be long, challenging, and lonely, despite being surrounded by upbeat, supportive people. Professional care-givers, family, and friends try to be sympathetic. But many of them are unable to fully understand what it is like to walk in your shoes, forcing yourself to engage in simple functional tasks that HURT

LIKE HELL when you try to do them. But force yourself, you must. The only other alternative is to spend the day sitting in a wheel chair with your head down, dozing and sleeping, slipping further and further away from life, waiting for God to put an end to your suffering. HURT LIKE HELL is a three-word description connecting how the "Being Old" sufferer feels and the final destination Old Scratch intends for those whom he can lure into despair.

The absence of debilitating pain is the ordinary state for the large majority of old people. They may experience stiffness, throbbing, stabbing sensations, and minor aches from time to time. But these can be lessened by applying homemade remedies (an ice pack or heating pad) and taking over-the-counter and prescription medications. While they experience some discomfort, this generally doesn't interfere with their ability to be congenial and to independently perform their daily activities.

Many old people do not escape the ravaging chronic pain, which knocks them out of the box and forces them onto the sidelines. "Why me?" the sufferer asks. "What did I do to deserve such punishment?" These thoughts can easily lead to envy of the more fortunate— envious of even those whom Christ called "evil doers" who prosper. An intense and constant self-pity, fueled by the belief that one has been unfairly singled out by a God Who has arbitrarily stuck him with "the short end of the stick," soon follows. The sufferer's self-pity, frustration, and anger only intensifies when his prayers for relief seem to be unanswered, believing this is further evidence that God has abandoned him.

It is at these times, when the "Being Old" sufferer is in a weakened spiritual condition, that Old Scratch can tempt him to throw the Rosary beads aside, blaspheme, and cast the gift of life into the wind, wishing that he had never been born. The devil, at these moments, will engage in an all-out frontal assault to get the sufferer to renounce Christ—urging him to angrily and loudly proclaim that he will not serve Him any longer. As one can see, unless the "Being Old" sufferer has a plan, in which he can utilize the satisfactory value of his suffering for the salvation of his soul and the souls of his loved ones, Hell could easily become his fate.

Facing our own decline and maintaining our faith in God and His mercy can be a tough and lonely battle. Deriving meaning out of what Old Scratch tries to present as being senseless is of the utmost importance in order to prevent the damnation of our soul. To those who suffer with chronic pain, I would like to offer the following poem by John Milton on his blindness, which I found to be helpful in bringing some clarity and purpose to this life and death struggle.

Sonnet XVI

When I consider how my light is spent,
Ere half my days, in this dark world and wide,
And that one talent which is death to hide
Lodged with me useless, though my soul more bent
To serve therewith my master, and present
My true account, lest he, returning chide,
"Doth God exact day-labor, light denied?"
I fondly ask: but Patience, to prevent
Thy murmur, soon replies: "God doth not need
Either man's work or his own gifts: who best
Bear his mild yoke, they serve him best: his state
Is kingly-thousands at his bidding speed
And post o'er land and ocean without rest:
They also serve who only stand and wait."

As this poem points out, the loss of our human powers, reducing us to a totally dependent, immobile state, does not mean that we cannot nobly serve God—on the contrary. It is those "who only stand and wait"—those "who best bear his mild yoke, who serve him best." "How can this be?" the sufferer asks. "How can I, reduced to an immobile and miserable state, please God and best serve Him?" *By example* is the answer. The acceptance of God's will and serving Him faithfully creates a peace that radiates within us. This peace and inner radiance is not lost on those who witness our suffering and the practicing of our Catholic Faith in overcoming Old Scratch's temptation to despair. It is these "Being Old" sufferers—those who are patient in their time of trial, who bring glory to God and are most pleasing to Him. By our example, we can draw others closer to God and His love for mankind.

The morning can be particularly loathsome for the chronic pain sufferer. Knowing that another unpleasant day awaits him can be depressing to say the least. Unless one can craft a plan that gives purpose for carrying the seemingly meaningless crosses, which he will be forced to carry, waking up and beginning the day will be a curse rather than a blessing. If the sufferer hasn't given up on praying to God, the Morning Offering can be particularly important in helping him to prepare for the upcoming battle. Through his suffering, he has the opportunity to gain the grace to earn merit for himself and his loved ones by saying the Prayer of Saint Ignatius of Loyola, which is as follows:

> Behold, O Lord, I offer you my whole being and in particular all my thoughts, words, and actions, together with such crosses and contradictions as I may meet with in the course of this day. Give them, O Lord, Your blessing; may your divine Love animate them and may they tend to the greater honor and glory of your Sovereign Majesty. Amen.

As difficult as this is, especially when we are in pain, it is important to keep in mind that our suffering has a sanctifying value if we ask God to make this so. It can be offered as "payback" for our sins and the sins of our loved ones. The greater the suffering, the greater is the redemptive value. For those "who only stand and wait," their crosses are heavy. God, in His infinite justice and mercy, will generously reward them and those for whom they pray. Friends and family, who are languishing in Purgatory, will be most grateful for your suffering, which is offered for their swifter purgation. What greater service can we offer to God and our loved ones and all of mankind? In today's secular world, in which Purgatory is ignored and an "everybody goes to heaven" mentality prevails, praying for our loved ones through our suffering is needed now more than ever. Let us not shun the cross God has given us in our suffering. It is a sign of His predilection. By carrying it with joy, or, at least with patience, we reduce our own time in Purgatory and that of others in exile for whom we pray. (More on this in the coming chapter on "The Exaltation of the Holy Cross.")

While crafting and putting a spiritual plan into practice is of the utmost importance, there are pitfalls, which the "Being Old" sufferer is bound to encounter. Unless he is intellectually and emotionally prepared, the resolve to face and overcome these can quickly evaporate. For those sufferers whose chronic pain has reduced them to a state in which they "can only stand and wait," it is imperative to try to keep in mind that the acceptance and graceful carrying of God's cross is what is most pleasing to Him. This is easy to keep in the forefront of our thoughts when our body is in a calm or quiet state. When we are languishing in pain, however, such noble thinking can become easily muddled, while our senses are screaming for relief. Again, dealing with chronic pain every day of your "Being Old" life can take away your desire to live, usurp your dignity, and weaken you to the point of despair. We can pray incessantly, but these prayers may never seem to be answered. Anxiety, frustration, and depression can fill our days. Hence, crafting a plan so that our life has purpose is essential for our emotional and spiritual survival.

There is another significant pitfall, of which the "Being Old" sufferer must be aware. It is important to realize that there will never be enough human compassion to fill the void now facing him. In fact, the seemingly insensitivity of other people to his suffering can become a major irritation in his relationships with them. "Can't they see I am suffering without having to be told that I am in pain?" he asks. "Are they so hard-headed they are unable to see that I need help without having to ask for it?" Their seeming lack of empathy can be particularly annoying, especially if they are family and friends with whom he has spent most of his life.

Another unpleasant reality, with which the "Being Old" sufferer must come to grips, is that even trained professional care-givers fall far short in their ability to empathize. To the chronic pain sufferer, this hardly makes any sense. "Almost anybody can be sympathetic to people who are obviously in pain, can't they?" Unfortunately, the answer to this question is NO. The world is populated with people who have varying degrees of sensitivity. Some can almost instinctively anticipate the sufferer's needs.

They don't have to be told that the patient is in pain. They sense this and respond accordingly. Why more care-givers are not proficient is an enigma for which there is no answer. Like every other profession, some persons are just more skilled then others, even though they have all had similar training. This is a fact of life we must learn to accept. The failure to do so will only increase our irritation and create strained relationships. Better that we accept their limitations and behave cordially toward them — a test of charity we might say, which can be offered to Our Lord. In our battle with chronic pain, we discover that despite our best efforts, saints we are not. And for those who take our Catholic Faith seriously, this also can be profoundly disappointing. Chronic pain forces us to see ourselves as we really are — frail and weak human beings far removed from those saintly stalwarts of the Faith, who carried their crosses in heroic fashion.

So what is the answer for "Being Old" chronic pain sufferers who may only stand and wait? There is only one answer that makes sense — faith in Christ Who promised us, "Behold I am with you all days." Trust that He keeps His promises and will be with us in times of joy and sorrow, particularly in the latter. Trust that if we are faithful to Him, He will provide us, not with comfort necessarily, but the strength to set good example — the strength to endure in the face of adversity; graciously smiling when we are filled with sadness; performing simple acts of charity; and providing encouragement and speaking kindly to those around us. And, most importantly, trust that if we are patient, He will infuse us with the necessary grace to understand and carry out His plan as He intended. Only this will remove the frustration, resentment, sadness, and self-pity, which could easily dominate our lives. Only this will lead us to a true love of Our Lord and bring about the inner peace, which will enable us to earn merit for ourselves and those souls for whom we pray. This is the stuff of which saints are made. Be aware that Old Scratch will try to exploit our suffering and turn it against our spiritual good. How is that? By tempting us to reject the cross God gifted to us by luring us into self-pity, frustration, and resentment.

They ("Being Old" pain sufferers) also serve who only stand and wait Part 2

In Part 1, the effects of chronic pain and how this can lead to despair and the loss of our soul were emphasized. Millions of human beings, young and "Being Old" alike suffer with illnesses, for which there are no cures. Many suffer with diseases that worsen with the passage of time. Their demise is slow and painful and the continuation of their suffering seems to serve no purpose. It is at these times that euthanasia and assisted suicide will appear to be attractive alternatives.

If the chronic pain sufferer is an atheist, the chances are that he or she will view suffering as being meaningless. To them, euthanasia and assisted suicide make perfect sense rather than living a life with pain that never ceases. "What difference does it make if I decide to kill myself?" the atheist would ask. "At least I will end this needless suffering. It's my life and I have the right to choose when I wish to end it." If our obligation to God and the loss of our soul is brought up, the atheist might continue to justify suicide by saying: "If there is a God as you say there is and He is all-merciful, He would certainly understand why I decided to kill myself. You said that I could go to Hell if I committed suicide. Yet, you say that God is good. How could a good God send His creatures to a place like that, especially when they have already suffered so much?" Even those "Being Old" chronic pain sufferers, who believe in God and the immortality of their soul, are bound to be plagued by such questions and thoughts. Unchallenged thinking of this nature is fertile ground on which Old Scratch can plant the seeds of despair, leading to eternal hell fire.

The reader will recall John Milton's poem on his blindness in which he stated: "They also serve who only stand and wait" and it is those "who best bear his mild yoke who serve him best." These are hard sayings, which are difficult to put into practice, especially when one is incapacitated. Concentrating and praying silently, simple acts of charity, setting good example, and remembering to offer the suffering for our sins and those of our loved ones who may be languishing in Purgatory are the right paths to follow. Graciously accepting God's cross, however, and trusting in His benevolence is a tough nut to swallow, particularly when you are in a weakened condition. It is at these moments that Old Scratch will be bending your ear about the uselessness of pain and God's mean-spirited unwillingness to take your cross away, especially when He has the power to do so.

For the "Being Old" sufferer, it is important to remember that the devil is called the Father of Lies for good reason. The clever manipulation of words, half-truths, and exaggeration are skillfully employed by him, making that which is false appear to be true. Isn't this how he lured the unsuspecting Eve into eating the forbidden fruit from the Tree of the Knowledge of Good and Evil? The promises made by the Father of Lies fell far short of Eve's expectations. Yet, these words, which so smoothly rolled off of his forked tongue, seemed reasonable at that time. Keep in mind that the Father of Lies will spin a yarn, especially designed to lure you away from God and into his clutches. He will pretend to be your advocate, and make it appear that God has abandoned you. These are the tricks of his trade.

"How will the Father of Lies try to lure me away from God?" the "Being Old" sufferer might ask. "What could he say about my chronic pain, which might lead to despair and arouse hatred within me for God and His Church?" There are a number of thoughts, which the Father of Lies will plant and nurture in your mind in order to weaken your resolve, arouse your indignation, and lose the desire to live. Some examples of these are as follows:

- First and foremost Old Scratch will try to convince you that you are a burden to family, friends, and those persons who are responsible for your care. Because you are unable to function independently, he will strongly suggest that you are a drain on their time, money, and resources. Most people take pride in being able to function independently. They can easily feel worthless when they are no longer able to do so. Thinking and repeatedly turning such thoughts over in your mind can only lead to self-hatred and despair.

- The chronic maladies, which cause us to suffer, can be inflicted upon us even though we have lived a moral life and practiced good health habits. The Father of Lies will point this out, focusing on its unfairness. He will especially draw your attention to those who behave immorally and eat, smoke, and drink to excess. Yet they may have no health problems and are prosperous. The rumination of such thoughts can not only lead to envy, hatred, and wishing ill will on others. Anger, resentment, and self-pity are the bitter fruits of such thinking.

- None of us had any choice about being born into this world. This was God's decision. The chronic pain that is inflicted upon us is also not of our choosing. Old Scratch will emphasize these facts, pointing out that if we had known that our life was to be so miserable, we might have chosen not to be born. The Father of Lies will raise the question: "Shouldn't the sufferer, who is the victim, have had the right to make that choice?" If the answer is YES, then rebellion fueled by feelings of intense anger is bound to dominate your thinking. This certainly will be pleasing to Old Scratch in his quest to capture your soul.

- The Father of Lies will taunt you about the futility of prayers, in which you ask God to relieve your suffering. He will concede that miracles have occurred at Lourdes and Fatima — occasionally a few people are cured. However, the odds of this happening are tantamount to trying to win the lottery. The large majority of persons who pray and travel to those sites where miracles have occurred, leave with no changes in their physical condition. "Why should this be any different for you?" the Father of Lies will ask. He will then emphasize that your past prayers have been fruitless and continuing to pray to an unfeeling God is pointless. Old Scratch knows that such thinking stokes up the fire of hopelessness, which can lead you into Hell.

- The Father of Lies will continue to remind you that the overriding majority of people, including the elderly, are healthy and able to function independently. He will point to those people, who are much older than you, but can still play tennis, travel, and engage in a wide variety of physical and social activities. He will suggest that your weakened condition and dependence on others means you are inferior and of much less value than those who are active, productive, and involved with family, friends, and in the community. Such thinking, if unchecked, will lead to self-pity, discontent, and envy.

- The unfairness of life and the fact that you have "drawn the short end of the stick" in comparison to others is an ongoing theme, which Old Scratch will pummel you with every day of your remaining life. If this thinking goes unchecked, you can easily behave rudely and become annoyed with family, friends, and care-givers who act cheerfully in your presence. "Are they so stupid they can't see that I am in pain?" you might ask yourself. "Can't they understand that I am suffering unfairly? How can they act so upbeat, when I, through no fault of my own, am so miserable?" Although you might not complain openly, your non-verbal behavior will convey that you perceive them as being unsympathetic and you would prefer to be left alone. Such thinking and behavior will further draw you away from family, friends, and those who care for you. You will then feel more isolated, alone, and unloved, another bedrock leading to greater resentment and eventual despair.

- As repeatedly emphasized, offering our suffering to expiate the temporal punishment due to our sins and for those in Purgatory can be a powerful incentive for nobly carrying the cross that Christ has placed on our shoulders. Our deceased loved ones can no longer earn merit. Therefore, they are powerless to reduce their own time in this place of intense chastisement. Carrying our cross and offering this for their remediation can significantly alter their sentence, bringing them closer to God and Heaven. For this, the suffering souls will be eternally grateful. While this goal is a noble one, expect Old Scratch to remind you that this is the twenty-first century, not the middle ages when people believed that Purgatory really existed. He will cite modern theologians and heretics who will say that Purgatory is a mythical creation of the past. Only foolish, ill-informed, and uneducated people would believe in such Dantesque nonsense.

A good current example of the preceding was the very popular and clever, comedic play, written by Vicki Quade, called *Late Nite Catechism*, which used a nun character to poke fun at the doctrine of Purgatory (and other Catholic things). Quade, oddly enough, is personally quite fond of Catholic sisters, so much so that she used the proceeds from the play (two million dollars in the 1994 Chicago run) to help fund Catholic sisters. A slick idea, the teacher, with pointer and blackboard, used the audience (with cued plants of course) as the class, the "Saint Bruno Adult Catechism Class." The name, Bruno, fit in with the acerbic (ha, ha) full-habited (naturally) teacher. Again, keep in mind that Old Scratch will suggest if you believe in Purgatory, you should consider yourself to be a moron. The devil's purpose is to make you believe that you are stupid. He will try to discourage you so that you will reject carrying your cross, and cast aside your spiritual commitment to those loved ones who are counting on you. Rather than being other-centered, he wants you to be self-centered, focusing on the needlessness of worldly suffering and how this has been unfairly inflicted upon you. Creating feelings of bitterness, resentment, and more self-pity within you is his goal. These will lead you to Hell.

- Old Scratch has not only been called the Father of Lies, but the Prince of the World for good reason as well. As the prayer to Saint Michael the Archangel states, the devil "prowls throughout the world seeking the ruin of souls." In order to achieve this objective, he tries to persuade his victims to focus on the present and bettering their lives as long as they are alive on planet earth. Jesus Christ, His Church, Heaven, Hell, Limbo, Purgatory, the eternity of the soul, and the final judgment are mocked and ridiculed by him. When you are suffering and crying out for relief, the Prince of the World will try to increase your pain by asking you questions such as, "Where is your God now that you need him? If He is so merciful, why doesn't He release you from this terrible pain?" It is during these times when your Faith will be tested to the utmost. If he can snatch away your Faith and break you spiritually, he will then leave you in a hopeless state. Perhaps he could convince you to commit suicide — he will promise that this will terminate your suffering—at least in this world—in the "here and now."

- Lastly, "Being Old" pain sufferers, who have been placed in nursing homes, are prime targets for the Father of Lies, especially if they have been loving and responsible parents during their children's formative and adult years. Elderly sufferers will be told by Old Scratch that because they can no longer independently care for themselves, their children view them as a burden. If they really loved Mom and Dad, they would take them into their homes, rather than send them off to a "warehouse," in which strangers are paid to look after their welfare. Old Scratch will put this thought in their mind, as they stare out the window, all alone, ruminating about how much they have done for their children in the years gone by. Now that they are incapacitated, their dedication and sacrifices are given short shrift and ignored. Nurturing such thoughts will lead to marked resentment directed toward their children and possibly extended family members as well. Moreover, the elderly sufferer will feel abandoned, isolated, and alone. Thoughts that their children really love their parents and have placed them in a nursing home out of necessity will be debunked by Old Scratch. He will insist that the elderly sufferer has been discarded. This will then lead to the fostering of family discord. The loss of all hope would soon follow. Perhaps Old Scratch could now influence the elderly sufferer to consider euthanasia. Again, the Father of Lies would promise that this would end all of his or her suffering—at least their suffering here on earth.

In conclusion, suffering with chronic pain has been and always will continue to be an integral part of human history. There are those who argue that we "put down" dogs, cats, horses, and other animals to relieve their pain. Yet we allow human beings to suffer needlessly—suffering with degenerative diseases that only worsen with the passage of time. Why not extend the same privilege to our fellow brothers and sisters who are in the "Being Old" stage of life, especially for those whose prolonged agony is unlikely to improve? Euthanasia and assisted suicide, they would insist, would be the most humane solution to this problem. "Death with dignity" would be their mantra.

If we are simply animals without an immortal soul, the proponents of euthanasia and assisted suicide would have a good case. Life, in their view, would terminate at the point of their demise on planet earth. If they have no belief in an afterlife and a God Who will exact a final judgment on how they lived their lives, this even strengthens their position. Chronic pain and the suffering associated with it would seem to be needless, especially if there was no

Supreme Being and no afterlife, in which one would be held accountable for his or her actions.

It is the spiritual component governing our lives here on earth that gives meaning to human suffering. In a world filled with corruption, willingly carrying our cross can make restitution for our sins and for the sins of those in Purgatory who are relying on our prayers to help them. This point is particularly important in light of the fact that modern Catholics have become increasingly more presumptuous in their thinking. Because God is all-merciful, they fail to recognize that He is all-just as well. Moreover, He has warned us that we will be held accountable for every idle word before entering Heaven. Hence, offering our suffering for the relief of those souls in Purgatory is more important than ever. Graciously carrying our cross with this purpose in mind will require that we try to behave like saints. Some say that this is impossible. But is it, especially when our loved ones, who are no longer in the flesh, are counting on us? Only we can answer this question, and only we can muster up the faith and courage making this possible.

Unfortunately, there is no other sensible alternative unless we follow the path, which Old Scratch and his minions have crafted for us. The choice is ours. We can put our trust in God or the Prince of the World and those unwitting fellow travelers who follow him. There is no "gray" area or point in between. As Christ said, "You are either with Me or against Me." This is the choice that we are required to make. If we decide to follow God's plan, the suffering that we must endure will be difficult. As stressed previously, we will be assaulted by the devil, who will promise us relief if we take the wide, not the narrow road. Those of us, who have been taught the Catholic Faith, know better. It is the latter, not the former road, which will lead us and those for whom we pray into paradise.

They ("Being Old" pain sufferers) also serve who only stand and wait
Part 3

In Parts 1 and 2, the importance of offering our suffering for the atonement of our sins and those of our loved ones, whether they are still in the flesh or in Purgatory, was emphasized. This was presented as the most meaningful alternative for managing chronic pain. It provides the "Being Old" sufferer with an iron-clad purpose for accepting their pain, and it serves as a powerful motivator for making prayerful use of the time God has allotted to him or her. The suffering offered to God strengthens us spiritually for our battle in "the here and now." Moreover, this offering, which we make in the present life, lasts for all eternity. In other words, the restitution for sin that we offer to God will last forever, long after our bodies have turned to dust.

The importance of willfully accepting the cross that the "Being Old" sufferer offers to God should not be overlooked. It provides the sufferer with the emotional and spiritual strength to tolerate the chronic pain and helps to override the bodily agony, which is likely to intensify, especially if Old Scratch is harassing you while you are in a weakened state.

The preceding might be compared to an ad that was popular several decades ago when Father Edward Flanagan opened an orphanage in Omaha, Nebraska, called Boys Town, a facility for wayward and delinquent youth. The ad showed a priest and a boy who is carrying an exhausted lad on his back after a long journey to the orphanage. The priest comments on how heavy a burden this must have been. The boy's classic response was: "Oh, he's not heavy Father, he's my brother." This is a fine example which demonstrated how love overcame any pain that this young man might have been experiencing. It also reminds us that if we trust in God and love our family and friends — really love them and care about the salvation of their souls — this can lighten our burden and enable us to carry our cross with the dignity that God intended.

In today's anti-Christian climate, there are legions of people who would disagree and openly mock the notion that suffering with chronic pain has any redeeming value. Chronic pain sufferers "who only stand and wait" are viewed as "useless eaters," using up resources and space in our over-populated planet. Better they be euthanized or assisted in committing suicide in order to solve this problem. If there was ever to be a utopia here on earth, these pundits would argue that man, not God, would create it. Moreover, they would point out that strong people, who are committed to a worldly cause, have within themselves those inner resources to remain productive despite being plagued with chronic pain. Strength of character and unswerving dedication enable them to override their suffering. God and His grace are not necessary.

These so-called intellectuals, who support the above, have a point. There are those persons, who despite being in poor health, are able to work diligently and productively, even though they experience chronic pain. Their dedication to a worldly cause can override their pain as they persist in their quest to build a utopia here on earth. In the end, however, they, too, will lose their human powers and become one of those "who only stand and wait." Death will soon follow. No one escapes this fate. They will then stand before God and face their final judgment. While they had the strength to work despite their ill-health, God will determine the value of their efforts. The world may honor them by constructing a statue, building, or memorial in their name. But what will this matter when they are judged by an all-just God Who will reward or punish them for eternity? It is the "Being Old" sufferers who may be required to carry the heaviest crosses. Therefore, addressing and answering the preceding question is of the utmost importance. The choices that we make and the salvation of our soul and the souls of our loved ones will depend on our answer.

For those who suffer with chronic pain, one final point should be taken into consideration. The sorrow that we experience in this world is only for a short time, which Christ described as being "a little while" (Gospel of Saint John 16:16-22) in comparison to eternity. Christ points out that when our time for suffering has come, it is natural to be sad and fearful. However, if we endure and cope with the pain as Our Lord intended, the suffering will pass and great joy, which can never be taken away from us, will follow. The following are Christ words:

> Amen, amen I say to you, that you shall weep and lament, but the world shall rejoice; and you shall be sorrowful, but your sorrow shall be turned into joy. A woman who is about to give birth has sorrow, because her hour has come. But when she has brought forth the child, she no longer remembers the anguish, for her joy that a man is born into the world. And you [Christ's disciples] therefore have sorrow now; but I will see you again, and your heart shall rejoice, and your joy no one shall take from you (John 16:20-22).

For the "Being Old" sufferer, the message is clear. If we carry our cross gracefully for "a little while," we will be rewarded with never-ending joy for eternity. This is Our Lord's promise, which must be kept in the forefront of our mind, especially when Old Scratch is telling us otherwise. Again, the salvation of our soul and the souls of those we love will depend on this.

Reflections on exaltation of the Holy Cross

September 14 is the day on which the Exaltation of the Holy Cross is celebrated. For some reason, this great feast day has caused me to reflect on it more deeply now than I have in the past. Perhaps it is the combination of "Being Old" and ill-health that has brought this about. Whatever the reason, like all Catholics who were born and reared in the 1940s and 50s, I learned to make the Sign of the Cross at an early age and I was taught that Catholics were supposed to carry their crosses gracefully—whining and complaining were shunned upon. This was an important part of my life and will continue to be so until the day I die.

Many "Being Old" generational Catholics begin the day with the Sign of the Cross. We sign ourselves before and after meals, at various moments throughout the day, and as a last act before going to sleep at night. If you watch a professional baseball game, you may see a batter, who is often of Hispanic descent, make the Sign of the Cross before entering the batter's box. If he gets a hit, making the Sign of the Cross as an act of thanksgiving to Our Lord, may follow. Like a professional baseball player, some of us might make the Sign of the Cross before facing a personal challenge about to arise in the course of the day. For those of us who attend the traditional Latin Mass, the signing of the cross and the genuflections before it are ever present. The exaltation of the Holy Cross is not only striking, but it fills us with feelings of intense joy.

While making the Sign of the Cross is uplifting, the thoughts of carrying a real cross are not joyful. Carrying a cross means that pain will be inflicted upon us, intense and sustaining pain of both a physical and mental nature. Being given a cross, although in truth a sign of God's love, can also be a punishment for past sins. It is "payback"—a debt—that we owe to Our Lord for violating His Laws. The full meaning of what this involves can only be understood by reflecting on the life of Jesus Christ and the suffering that He endured to redeem us. We need to call to mind the First Sorrowful Mystery of the Rosary—"the Agony in the Garden." Try to picture Our Lord, alone with His thoughts before He was arrested and brought to trial. He knew in explicit detail what He would soon be facing, the pain, the abandonment, and the humiliation. This would culminate in being nailed to a wooden cross and mocked unmercifully by those for whom He was sacrificing His life. No appreciation or pity was shown here—not a speck of compassion for "the Lamb of God, You who take away the sins of the world"—not a bit of sympathy for Our Lord, except from His dear mother, some holy women, and Saint John the Apostle.

After telling His disciples He would soon be crucified and rebuking Peter who opposed this revelation, Jesus said to His disciples,

> If anyone wishes to come after Me, let him deny himself, and take up his cross, and follow Me. For he who would save his life shall lose it; but he who loses his life for My sake will find it. For what does it profit a man, if he gains the whole world but suffers the loss of his soul? For the Son of Man is to come with angels and the glory of His Father, and then will render to everyone according to his conduct (Matthew 16:24-27).

Saint Matthew's Gospel points the way to Heaven. However, willingly carrying life's crosses is a hard sell. Our natural inclination is to minimize pain and to avoid as much suffering as possible. This is in marked contrast to what Christ and the great saints had in mind. The great saints believed that their cross was a gift of love given to them by Our Lord. Because of the cross' power of expiation, these holy men and women EMBRACED their crosses, rather than try to escape or avoid them. Imagine this being preached from the pulpit in today's modern Church and the reaction of those in attendance. The importance of gracefully carrying the cross and its sanctifying value has decreased markedly over the past half-century. This has been replaced by an increase in pleasure-seeking secularism and the "celebrating of life" on earth. These have become the new gospel.

Saint Paul, in his First Epistle to the Corinthians (1:17-25), warned us of this "foolishness" two thousand years ago:

> Brethren: Christ did not send me to baptize, but to preach the gospel, not with the wisdom of words, lest the cross be made void. For the doctrine of the Cross is foolishness to those who perish, but to those who are saved, that is to us, it is the power of God.

Today more than ever, willingly accepting one's crosses, never mind embracing them, is ignored, ridiculed, and rejected. Who in their right mind would freely choose to seek out and joyfully accept horrific crosses such as poverty, poor health, and human disrespect? And those few who are willing to do so—like the great saints—would be judged as eccentric at best or outright lunatics, who have lost touch with reality, at worst. Yet the great saints considered the cross as a sign of being loved by God. They believed that the heavier the cross, the greater was the love Our Lord had for him or her.

Ordinary "Being Old" folks and younger men and women look at carrying crosses differently. We often do all that we can to avoid life's adversities. If we are unable to escape from these, we might begrudgingly accept our fate, resigning ourselves to the fact that this is God's will. With a stiff upper lip, we plod on, asking Our Lord for mercy and the strength to overcome the trials set before us. Deep down inside many of us wish that we could do better than this. Simply resigning ourselves to the will of God is hardly enough — the bare minimum. We really wish that we could act like those saints who came before us. Again, who among us doesn't aspire to emulate the great saints, gracefully and joyfully EMBRACING our cross and setting the perfect example on how we should live and die?

Who wants to look weak to the people around us, especially to those who are non-Catholics and those who no longer practice the Catholic Faith. If you are a traditional Catholic, the chances are good that you will know friends and family who pick and choose what they wish to believe. It is at these most trying times that our Faith should give us the strength to gracefully endure.

Non-Catholics, lukewarm Catholics, and Catholic "drop-outs" know this. This can be a struggle for us "Being Old" Catholics — a struggle with the most dangerous of Capital Sins — the sin of pride. Oh, so badly, we want to set a good example! Oh, so badly, we want to show those around us that being a traditional Catholic does make a difference — that Jesus Christ and Our Blessed Mother are filling us with the grace to not only carry our cross, but to thrive and behave radiantly as well. Needless to say, our pride, if left unchecked, can do more harm than good in carrying Christ's message to those who have abandoned or no longer have confidence in the Catholic Church.

As the years pass and we finally arrive at the "Being Old" stage of life, the chances are that our crosses will increase and intensify. Our Lord, in His way, is preparing us to sever our attachments and to disengage from the world. It is at this time that we can expect Old Scratch to turn up the heat in his final attempt to capture our soul. As stressed throughout this book, for those of us who reach the "golden years," trying to tempt us to despair will be one of Old Scratch's favorite tactics.

In the Introduction, I pointed to the work of Erik Erikson, a well-known developmental psychologist, who postulated that human beings pass through several stages, each of which presents a critical psychosocial conflict to be resolved. The favorable resolution of each conflict not only facilitates our mental health, but makes it less likely that we will bring "baggage" from the past with us as we progress into the next stage. Interestingly, Erikson identified ego integrity versus despair as the last psychosocial conflict to be resolved in our final stage of life (old age being sixty-five plus years of age). If we perceive our life as having been purposeful and productive, Erikson contends that a sense of satisfaction and the courage to face death will follow. If we perceive ourselves as having failed, however, depression and hopelessness will become our bedfellows. Of course, as mentioned previously, Erikson's approach leading to the final resolution of this last psychosocial conflict is a secular and limited one. God and the Catholic Church do not enter into this equation.

The good news for us is that thanks to our Catholic heritage, the Holy Cross of Jesus Christ will always trump despair. Why? Because Our Lord promised that this would be so. Not only did He die for our sins, but He provided us with an arsenal of spiritual weaponry, that if used as He intended, guarantees that we will be victorious over Old Scratch and his minions. The cross and the suffering attached to it are a most powerful propitiatory weapon in the battle to save souls. It is up to us, however, to carry it accordingly.

> *Saint John of the Cross, Doctor of the Catholic Church (+1591), who suffered much physical and mental anguish, pray for us.*

A plea to "Being Old" sufferers from the souls in Purgatory

Throughout this book, the importance of praying for the souls in Purgatory will be repeatedly emphasized. The existence of Purgatory is given short shrift in today's presumptuous society. Rather, many Catholics, like their fellow Protestants, have come to believe that deceased relatives and friends have gone straight to Heaven. Faith alone, without good works, is all that is needed to be saved. Or, on the other hand, good works is all that is necessary for salvation, not divine and Catholic Faith. Whether the deceased was in a state of mortal or venial sin at the time of death is irrelevant. The thought that relatives and friends would be sentenced to Purgatory, requiring that their souls be purified by fire, would be anathema to those who overly focus on Our Lord's compassion. They fail to recognize the fact that Our Lord is all-just as well. It is His justice that will determine whether our souls will be damned or saved when we stand before Him following our last breath.

Our Lord did not say that the road to Heaven would be a wide one. Simply declaring that "I believe in Jesus Christ" and maintaining one's faith would hardly be enough to enter paradise immediately after death. Rather, Our Lord insisted that in order to enter the Kingdom of Heaven, our soul must be pure, perfect, and unblemished—cleansed from even the most minor imperfection. For those who die in grace, this purification, as you know, is done in Purgatory. Consider Our Lord's words from the Gospel of Saint Matthew (5:17-19):

> Do not think that I have come to destroy the Law or the Prophets. I have not come to destroy, but to fulfill. For I say amen to you, till heaven and earth pass away, not one jot or one tittle shall be lost from the Law till all things have become accomplished. Therefore whoever does away with one of these least Commandments, and so teaches men, shall be called least in the kingdom of heaven, but whoever carries them out and teaches them, he shall be called great in the kingdom of heaven.

Do the preceding words sound like those of a God who would overlook small but voluntary sins, ignore minor rule violations, or accept slightly "spoiled goods" into the House of His Father? Jesus Christ was perfect and He challenged His disciples to strive for perfection, "Be you therefore perfect as your heavenly Father is perfect" (Matthew 5:48). Christ loved sinners but hated sin, which violated His Law. He never said that fulfilling the letter and spirit of the Law would ever be easy. Rather, He asks us "to pick up your cross and follow Me."

While the preceding emphasizes God's justice and the importance of fulfilling His Laws as He intended, we should not lose sight of the fact that as long as we are alive on earth, God mercifully provides us with sufficient grace to save our soul. By cooperating with His grace, we can not only earn merit for ourselves, but the merit we earn through our prayers and suffering can be offered as payment to shorten the sentence of our loved ones who are in Purgatory. What a blessing this is for these poor suffering souls, being purified and cleansed and anticipating the day when they will enter the Kingdom of Heaven. Our offerings give them consolation. What better way is there to show our benefactors the gratitude for the good that they may have done for us when we shared life with them on earth? Isn't this the kind of charitable act that Jesus Christ would expect, especially from those of us "Being Old" sufferers who were reared in the true Catholic Faith and were once taught how much the suffering souls in Purgatory depended on our prayers?

It is important to keep in mind that merit for ourselves and our deceased loved ones can only be earned while we have life in this world. Again, once the soul leaves the body and we stand before God, the opportunity to earn merit will be over and we will be judged by the record that we left behind while living on earth. There will be no second chance to make restitution for the remission of past sins. Rather, we will be required to endure the cleansing fire of Purgatory without any reduction in our sentence unless someone, who is still alive on planet earth, prays for us. This is not to say that those who have been devoted to Our Lady, her Rosary, and have fulfilled the five consecutive First Saturday devotions will not have a reduced sentence. (The Reader will note in the upcoming chapter on the Rosary the great promises attached to the Rosary and First Saturday devotions.)

For those Catholics who attend the Novus Ordo, the preceding is particularly significant. The traditional importance of saying penitential prayers and the offering of a Requiem Mass with black vestments are often overlooked. Rather, the deceased person's life here on earth is "celebrated." Perhaps a poster board is made, which is filled with photos of the deceased when he or she was alive, during happier times. If there is a wake, the poster board is located in a prominent place for everyone to see. In order to enhance the celebration, pictures, trinkets, and other worldly paraphernalia, to which the deceased had a sentimental attachment, are placed in the open casket. These, like the poster board photos, serve as a reminder of happier times, when the deceased was in the prime of his or her life and fully engaged in worldly endeavors. Again, the items in the open casket and their relevance to the deceased's life on earth rather than the current state of his or her soul become the focal point of attention.

As an aside, I can recall attending a wake in which racing forms were placed in the deceased's casket. During his retirement years, he enjoyed going to the track and betting on the horse races. This, of course, became the topic of light, carefree conversation. All I could think of was this man standing before Our Lord clutching these racing forms in his hands during the judgment, a most frightening prospect indeed. Instead of saying the Sorrowful Mysteries of the Holy Rosary, the room was filled with social chatter. He was described as being a fun-loving "good person" who was now "in a better place," reunited with other loved ones in Heaven. The thought that his soul might be condemned to Hell or that he would be required to suffer in Purgatory was far removed from anyone's mind.

To add to the above, a Mass of Christian Burial with white vestments instead of a Requiem Mass with black vestments was offered. Again, in the Novus Ordo, white trumps black so the "celebration" of the deceased's life on earth can continue. Perhaps a family member or friend will give the eulogy, extolling the deceased's virtues, exaggerating his goodness. After all, we are here to celebrate the deceased's life on earth. Who would want to throw a wet blanket on such a celebration by suggesting that the deceased may need our prayers, now more than ever?

Now that I am in the "Being Old" stage of my life, I often think of my deceased parents, relatives, and friends. Do we not hear the souls in Purgatory pleading for our help? We know that they are, by the Church's teaching. Yet their crying out for mercy goes unheeded. Today's "everybody goes to heaven" mentality has caused us to become so spiritually dulled we can no longer hear the pleading of the suffering souls, believing rather that penitential prayers and Masses are unnecessary. How can we let their pleas go unnoticed and consider ourselves to be a merciful people? The answer to this question is obvious. Penitential prayers and Masses for the faithful departed should be restored and elevated to their former level of importance. These charitable acts of mercy will serve as a most efficacious benefit, for which the suffering souls will be truly thankful. Not only are they thankful for our help in relieving them now, but in gratitude they can pray for us too, although not for themselves. And their prayers for us when they enter Heaven will be even more efficacious.

Lastly, it is up to us — "Being Old" Catholics — to hear the pleas of friends and relatives who may be languishing in Purgatory. Pain and suffering can and often are the greatest when we are near the end of our life and our human powers are declining — these are the heaviest of crosses, which Our Lord is asking us to bear. What greater gift can we give to those deceased persons whom we loved, than to offer our suffering on their behalf!

Reflections on seemingly unanswered prayers

Now that I am in the "Being Old" stage of life, the wise use of my time is becoming increasingly more precious. God, in His mercy, has granted me the time to pray and put my life in order. How I use this gift is up to me. While we know that God has promised to answer our prayers, praying can be a frustrating experience. Our Lord said that if we asked the Father for anything in His name, our wish would be granted, "Ask and you shall receive; seek and you shall find; knock and it shall be opened to you" (Luke 11:9). But so many times the sufferer's prayers may appear to go unanswered. They continually ask for relief, which seemingly is not forthcoming, and they repeatedly knock on a door that never seems to open.

Whoever said that growing old wasn't for the fainthearted, hit the nail on the head, particularly if your health is poor and you suffer with chronic pain or a consuming and debilitating disease. Who among us has not prayed for relief only to find that our cries for help seem to fall on deaf ears. This doesn't stop the faithful from continuing to pray, however. Those, who are truly faithful, realize that they need to do more — doing more is the remedy. They need to pray more Rosaries, attend Mass more frequently, and engage in more charitable acts to help the less fortunate. Again, they ask in the name of Our Lord, Jesus Christ, that their petition be granted. But alas! Despite their increased effort, nothing appears to change.

How depressing this seemingly unending cycle can be. Some will say that there are many others far worse off than you, the sufferer. Who could deny this? However, there is little solace to be found here. Just because other people are experiencing greater suffering isn't likely to make you feel better. One might reflect on the life of Saint Monica, who prayed for seventeen years, asking that her son, Saint Augustine, enter the Catholic Church. For seventeen years Saint Monica prayed before her wish was granted. Who among us believes that we have the strength to endure such a trial? There could be little solace to be found here as well. After all, we might rationalize: "Saint Monica is a canonized saint. We, on the other hand, are ordinary human beings. We are not saints, even though we would like to be so."

Some sufferers, if they have the resources, might travel to Lourdes or Fatima and petition Our Blessed Mother for relief. At the end of their journey, however, the overriding majority of these pilgrims remain uncured. They come to Lourdes and Fatima believing that Our Lady will take away their suffering. Yet, only a very few are granted their wish. Not being one of the chosen few can be most discouraging, especially if the petitioner has prayed and been loyal to Christ and His Church. Seemingly unanswered prayers and the absence of relief can tempt one to despair, the seeds of which are planted and nurtured in our soul by Old Scratch with the hope of weakening our faith and luring us into Hell.

In the quest to understand why many prayers seem to go unanswered, some real soul searching is in order. Periodic episodes of self-pity need to be put to rest; otherwise, the sufferer's prayer life will diminish and could eventually be lost. Despite having lived for more than three quarters of a century, I discovered that many of my past prayers have been like those of a child rather than a man. The words of Saint Paul in his First Epistle to the Corinthians come to mind:

> When I was a child; I spoke as a child; I understood as a child; I thought as a child. But when I became a man, I put away the things of a child… (13:11).

Many of my prayers, unlike those of a man, were like those of a child. I would make promises such as: "Oh God! If you will grant me this wish, I will go to Mass every day next week." I asked God for things that I thought would make me happy and bargained with Him accordingly. My main focus was on what I wanted, not on what God willed for me.

I grew up in a traditional Catholic family in the 1940s and 50s. As a boy, my prayers were filled with bargaining, trading, and asking Our Lord for "favors," which I thought were important at the time. My passion was playing baseball. Like many young boys, who lived during this era, I aspired to become a professional baseball player. I vividly recall praying to Our Lord asking Him to put "more pop" into my bat so that I could excel as a hitter and move to a higher level of competition.

During my early teenage years, I was competing with another young man for the batting championship. How important this was to me at the time. Oh! How badly I wanted that recognition. The night before the biggest game, I petitioned Our Blessed Mother for her help, saying three Rosaries in her honor. Lo and behold! My request was granted. I cranked out three hits in three trips to the plate — a perfect day, winning the batting title. Needless to say, this was an example of asking and thinking like a child. Our heavenly Father, like our good father here on earth, granted requests that made me momentarily happy. As long as He continued to answer my prayers, it made sense to me that I should keep petitioning Him. God did a lot of "favors" for me back then. I suspect that my child-like requests were granted more frequently than not. As a result, I developed a habit of asking, and of course expecting, that I would receive what I asked for.

Chasing the dream of becoming a professional baseball player soon vanished along with my early youth. I was no longer a child. Our Lord and Our Lady rightly expected me to "put away the things of a child" and to speak, understand, and act like a man. This meant asking God for things that would be pleasing to Him and would lead to the salvation of my soul. God made it clear that all earthly trappings, if they were necessary for helping us to fulfill His divine plan, will be given to us. In light of this, He expects that we should have absolute trust in Him and remain stalwart in our faith, especially when adversity arises. "Why?" you might ask. Because God is all-good—He can be counted upon to always keep His promises.

An example of the above appears in the Book of Kings. Most of us are familiar with the story of King Solomon, who was a loving and loyal subject of God. God appeared in a dream to King Solomon and said: "Ask for whatever you want Me to give you." Solomon then answered: "So give your servant a discerning heart to govern your people and to distinguish between good and evil" (3 Kings 3:9). Note that King Solomon did not ask for a long life, honor, wealth, the death of his enemies, or any other temporal rewards. He asked for wisdom, not personal gain. Needless to say, God was pleased with Solomon's answer. He, therefore, not only endowed Solomon with wisdom, but promised him a long life, honor, wealth, and such greatness "that in your [King Solomon's] lifetime you will have no equal among kings." Obviously, King Solomon had "put away the things of a child" and acted like a man of God.

The message of King Solomon is a clear one. It is up to us to discern what is pleasing to God and petition Him accordingly. Perhaps those things that we are requesting could be harmful to the salvation of our soul, if God granted them. There is an old saying, "Be careful what you wish for—you just might get it." How many times do we hear about those rich and famous people, who have everything life has to offer? Yet, they wreck their lives or commit suicide. By seemingly not answering our prayers, Our Lord may be doing us a great favor. However, in our spiritual blindness we whine like children, thinking that we know better than Him what is best for us. If we believe that Our Lord is not answering our prayers, then maybe some serious soul searching is in order. Maybe that which we are requesting from God is not pleasing to Him. By denying our petition, He might be really answering our prayers — some food for thought before we continue on the same dry course, leading to further disappointment.

So the question we need to address is, "What should we ask from Our Lord that would be pleasing to Him?" Putting our absolute faith in Him and His promise to answer our prayers would be a good place to start. Did Our Lord not encourage us?

> Have faith in God. Amen, I say to you, whoever says to this mountain, "Arise, and hurl yourself, into the sea" and does not waiver in his heart, but believes that whatever he says will be done, it will be done for him. Therefore I say to you, all things whatever you ask for in prayer, believe that you will receive, and they shall come to you (Mark 11:22-24).

In the preceding, Christ not only stresses the importance of a strong and unyielding faith, but He asks the penitent to "not waiver in his heart" when he prays. Being persistent is emphasized here. Those of us who become weak of heart can easily fall into self-pity, giving in to those immobilized feelings of despair when adversity arises. It is during these moments that the Father of Lies will fill your head with irrational thoughts, encouraging you to give up and follow him into Hell. Yes! Persistence, persistence, and more persistence! Again, Our Lord emphasized the importance of this virtue in the Gospel of Saint Luke (11:5-13):

> At that time Jesus said to His disciples: "Which of you will have a friend and shall go to him in the middle of the night and say to him 'Friend, lend me three loaves for a friend of mine has just come to me from a journey, and I have nothing to set before him,' and he from within should say, 'Do not disturb me; the door is now shut, and my children and I are in bed; I cannot get up to give to you?' I say to you, although he will not get up and give to him because he is his friend, yet because of his persistence, he will get up and give him all that he needs. And I say to you, ask and it shall be given to you; seek, and you shall find; knock and it will be opened to you. For everyone who asks receives; and he who seeks finds; and to him who knocks it shall be opened. But if one of you asks his father for a loaf, will he hand him a stone? or for a fish, will he for a fish, hand him a serpent? or if he asks for an egg, will he hand him a scorpion? Therefore, if you, evil as you are, know how to give good gifts to your children, how much more will your heavenly Father give the Good Spirit to those who ask Him."

As the preceding shows, an unwavering faith and persistence in its practice is what is pleasing to Our Lord. Placing total trust in His hands, with the explicit intention of fulfilling His will, is what He wants from us. This is the road leading to the answering of all of our prayers. When we have reached this pinnacle, we will have "put away the things of a child" and "put on the things of a man."

To those fellow "Being Old" sufferers, who are wrestling with the issue of seemingly unanswered prayers, I would once again like to recommend a prayer of Saint Ignatius of Loyola for your consideration:

> Take, O Lord, and receive my entire liberty, my memory, my understanding, and my whole will. All that I am and all that I possess You have given me. I surrender it all to You to be disposed of according to Your will. Give me only Your love and Your grace; with these I will be rich enough and desire nothing more.

Notice that Saint Ignatius only asks for Our Lord's love and grace. No earthly trappings are requested. Despite the shortness of this prayer, in my humble opinion, it is most pleasing to Our Lord.

As stressed previously, when one is in the midst of great suffering, asking for symptom relief rather than the strength to submit to God's will can be a difficult and most challenging task. It is at these moments that the Father of Lies will be doing his utmost to convince you to question Our Lord's veracity. Keep in mind the words of Saint Paul: "When I was a child, I spoke as a child…" Don't let Old Scratch trick you into exchanging a "man's prayers" for those of a child during these most trying times. Our Lord, unlike Old Scratch, keeps His promises.

"Being Old" reflections on "the way we were"

It has been fifty years since the closing of the Second Vatican Council on December 8, 1965, the Feast of the Immaculate Conception. I was twenty-six years old when the Council terminated. I had just returned to the United States after serving a two-year stint in the Peace Corps as a volunteer in Liberia, West Africa. This was before the bloody revolution leading to the overthrow of the Liberian government. I was an idealist back then. I was brought up in a solidly Catholic family, which produced one of the great Maryknoll priests of that time, Father Joseph Lavin. Father Joe was dubbed the "Iron Man of China" by the well-known historian Theodore White. His exploits in courageously opposing the Communists, when they rose to power in 1948, were legendary. Back then, if any soothsayer or prophet had told me what the moral climate would be like today and how markedly different this would be from the life that I had lived in my youthful years, I would have shouted, "NO WAY!"

I graduated from a Catholic high school and college, both of which still practiced the traditional Faith. Massachusetts, my home state, while being liberal, was influenced by a Church hierarchy and laity that stood strongly for Catholic principles and what we now call "family values." This was a time when a pastoral letter from the bishop was read from the pulpit and taken seriously. The thought that Massachusetts would be the first state to make homosexual "marriage" the law of the land would never have entered my mind or the minds of those cohorts of my generation. Who would have thought that something like this could ever happen! The year of 1965 was a high point for priestly vocations. According to official Church figures, there were 58,632 priests nationwide at this time. However, by 2014, this number sunk to 38,275, nearly a 35% decline in five decades!

In an article entitled "On the Bus: Vatican II and the Decline of Women Religious," Vincent Chiarello cited other statistics pointing to the abysmal decline of the Catholic Church over the past half-century (*Remnant Newspaper*, Nov. 30/Dec. 15, 2014, p. 1). Some of these are: (1) The nation-wide ratio of priests to parishioners had increased from 1 to 653 to 1 to 1,653 by the year 2010; (2) In Chiarello's home parish in Arlington, Virginia, this ratio was even more draconian, increasing from 1 to 874 to 1 to 1,958 by the year 2012; and (3) Most striking was the overwhelming, significant decline of women religious, plummeting from a high of 179,954 in the year 1965 to 49,883 by 2014—a marked drop of 75%. WOW! Who would have ever thought that those stalwart, dedicated nuns, the heart and soul of Catholic education, would one day be replaced by a lay administrative and teaching staff? NO WAY!

Chiarello made several other observations, which focused upon how much the Church has changed since the middle of the 1960s. In my youthful years, interest in and vocations to the foreign missions were booming. A family that produced a priest, particularly a missionary priest, was considered to be especially blessed, a crown jewel of that family we might say. As noted previously, recent figures show a marked decline in priestly vocations. However, this decline was even worse than reported given the fact that the remaining priests were becoming older and infirm, exacerbating the loss of needed clergy. This shortage has led to what Chiarello termed a "strange reversal." Whereas the United States used to send missionaries abroad to preach the Catholic Faith, we are now importing priests from Latin America, Asia, and Africa to fill understaffed parishes here at home. And the future looks bleak in this regard. Interestingly, India, not the United States, is producing the highest number of seminarians. Again, fifty years ago, I would have shouted from the housetops, "NO WAY!"

One other observation reported by Chiarello stuck out like a sore thumb. On January 7, 2015, twelve journalists were murdered by "Islam extremists" in broad daylight in Paris, France. To add insult to injury, on November 13 of this same year, another string of well-orchestrated terrorist attacks occurred in Paris, which resulted in the death of 130 innocent civilians. Needless to say, this brazen slaughter of unsuspecting victims was surprisingly shocking to say the least. NO WAY would this have been anticipated by us ordinary folks fifty years ago! But a lot has changed since then. In our "I'm okay, you're okay" social environment, we have ignored the writing of Hilaire Belloc, the great Catholic author, who in his book, *The Crusades: The World's Debate*, warned us that Islam was anything but the peaceful religion some make believe it to be. Rather, it is a religion that is committed to conquering and slaughtering those infidels who oppose them. History proves it and the Koran demands it.

France, the "eldest daughter" of the once Militant Catholic Church, held the Mohammedan jihadists in check in the years gone by. In 1950, it was estimated that there were 40,000 priests in France. Today there are less than 9,000. Mosques have replaced churches that were once Catholic, and Moslems are far more dedicated to Islam than many Catholics are to Jesus Christ and His Church. Who in the 1950s would have ever predicted that France, whose patron saint is Joan of Arc, would be threatened by the sword of Islam? Who would believe that Islamist terrorists would have the gall to video tape the decapitation of innocent victims and brazenly flaunt these sickening displays throughout the Western world? NO WAY!

With the ever decreasing decline of Catholic influence, the United States has devolved into a quagmire of spiritual and moral decay, which would have been shocking to those previous generations who were reared in the traditional Church. Consider the following notorious events that have taken place in the last five decades:

- The legalization of abortion and the sale of infant body parts. Abortion, the murdering of the unborn in the mother's womb, is a mortal sin that cries out to Heaven for vengeance. Who would have believed that the U.S. Supreme Court would judge this to be a Constitutional right intended by the Founding Fathers of our great nation?

- The repeal of laws prohibiting the cohabitation of unmarried couples. Young and even older people live together without bothering to marry. Scandal and shame once associated with this sinful behavior is no longer a deterrent.

- The repeal of the laws against sodomy. Civil unions between same-sex couples have become commonplace and "gay" marriage has become the law of the land. Homosexual behavior, which is a sin that cries out to Heaven for vengeance, is now celebrated in gay pride parades throughout the nation. Even the psychiatric community, which once labeled homosexuality as a mental disorder, now considers it to be "normal."

- The legalization of marijuana. The use of marijuana has been decriminalized. The harmful effects have been downplayed and it is now viewed as a recreational drug.

- The marked drop in Mass attendance since 1965. Many of today's Catholics no longer believe they have an obligation to attend Sunday Mass and that it is a mortal sin for failing to do so.

- The lack of belief in the Real Presence of Jesus Christ in the Consecrated Host and Chalice. Over half of today's Catholics believe that the Mass is a mere memorial meal commemorating the Paschal meal of the Last Supper, and that the Consecrated Host and Chalice of Wine are merely *symbolic* of the Body and Blood of Our Lord.

- The scandalous behavior of many priests and brothers, sexually disoriented usually, who have sexually abused and corrupted our youth, and the compliance of those bishops, who have covered up and lied about this matter. As a result, the Church has not only become financially devastated due to legal and settlement fees, but has lost its moral authority as well. There is no coincidence here that filthy sex-education programs have been corrupting the youth not only in the public school system but in Catholic schools as well. And this goes back to the sixties.

- The breakdown of the family structure and those values that supported this once hallowed societal unit. In today's society, the roles of mother and father are no longer clearly defined. Both parents work, and the care of children is being left to after-school programs and day care centers. The state and Federal governments have become more involved in the rearing and education of our children. Parents have been increasingly losing their authority to care for their offspring as they see fit.

This list of changes occurring over the past half-century could go on and on. When we contrast today with the 1940s and 50s, the differences between them is so blatant it is hard to believe that the latter had roots in the former. The obvious question arises: "How have we become so morally and spiritually dulled in such a short period of time?" Consider the following quote by the British author Dresden James, which provides us with an answer to this question:

> A truth's initial commotion is directly proportional to how deeply the lie is believed. It wasn't the world being round that agitated people, but [that] the world wasn't flat. When a well-packaged web of lies has been sold gradually to the masses over generations, the truth will seem utterly preposterous and its speaker a raving lunatic.

Who can deny that we have been gradually sold a "well-packaged web of lies" by many in the Church hierarchy, by politicians, and national leaders who should know better? The "masses over generations" have come to view that which was once sacred and true as "preposterous." Traditional Catholics have become the "raving lunatics," insisting that the Church founded by Our Lord is One, Holy, Catholic, and Apostolic and it is the only Church through which our immortal soul can be saved. It is the Traditionalists who insist that the dogmas of the Catholic Church are non-negotiable and will always be fixed in stone.

While the title of this chapter makes reference to the song popularized by Barbara Streisand in 1973, "The Way We Were" is more than entertainment. "The Way We Were" is meant to be a benchmark, a baseline from which those "Being Old" cohorts from my generation started on life's trek beginning in the 1940s to where we are today. By looking at this baseline and contrasting it with the present, we can assess our progress or lack thereof over the past five decades.

As noted previously, the differences between these two time periods are so stark it is hard to believe that the latter sprung from the former. What has brought this about? A profound change in our thinking, the way that we view life and its purpose has firmly taken hold. Our thoughts have been gradually shaped and molded so that we have come to believe that fiction is truth and truth is fiction. Virtue has become vice and vice virtue. Objective truth has been cast aside. Truth is now only subjective—that which is in the mind of the beholder, who makes it whatever he wants it to be. Instead of the mind receiving the truth, i.e., reality, the subjectivists create their own truth (falsehood) or reality, the will moving the intellect rather than the other way around. It was Saint Paul who warned us that this would happen:

> For there will come a time when they will not endure the sound doctrine; but having itching ears, will heap upon themselves teachers according to their own lusts, and they will turn away from hearing the truth and turn aside rather to fables (2 Timothy 4:1-8).

"The Way We Were" is a chronicle of events connecting the past with the present. Although the past is fixed, the future can bring about change if we choose to do so. As the preceding has emphasized, the currently "in your face" violations of Natural and Divine Law are an insult to and mockery of Our Lord, which should not be taken lightly. Through Our Blessed Mother, He has warned us of dire punishments if we continue to ignore His requests (e.g., consecration of Russia to the Immaculate Heart of Mary), dishonor Him, and violate His Commandments. The question arises: "How should we conduct ourselves in these seemingly hopeless times?" Again, Saint Paul offers the following: "But be watchful in all things, bear with tribulation patiently, work as a preacher of the gospel, fulfill your ministry" (2 Timothy 4:5). Saint Paul tells us that we must be preachers of the Catholic Faith, warning us to be "watchful in all things" lest we become deceived by false prophets and devoured by wolves in sheep's clothing. Tribulations must be dealt with patiently and we must persevere right to the end, thereby "fulfilling our ministry," as Our Lord intended.

For those "Being Old" sufferers who tend to become discouraged, it is important to keep in mind that God loves us and considers preaching His Gospel—"fulfilling our ministry"—to be of the highest priority, especially in these times in which His Church is being assailed by His enemies. When Old Scratch is tempting you and feelings of doubt begin to arise, consider Our Lord's words in His Sermon on the Mount:

> You are the salt of the earth. But if the salt loses its savor, wherewith shall it be salted? It is good for nothing anymore, but it must be cast out, and to be trodden by men. You are the light of the world. A city seated on a mountain cannot be hid. Neither do men light a candle and put it under a bushel, but upon a candlestick that it might shine to all that are in the house. So let your light shine before men, that they see your good works, and glorify your Father in heaven (Matthew 5:13-16).

Notice that Our Lord refers to His disciples as the "salt of the earth." Salt, during ancient times, was used as a preservative—an essential in sustaining life we might say. It was also important enough to be used as currency. In this parable, Christ is telling "the salt of the earth" that they have an important job to do. Without them (the salt of the earth) to preach His Gospel, the Faith will be lost and life will lose its purpose, its savor. It is up to "the salt of the earth" to keep this from happening. Moreover, Our Lord refers to His disciples as "the light of the world," whose duty is to "shine before men." By their example and "good works," they can teach their fellow men to glorify Our Father in Heaven and save their souls. What better compliment can us "Being Old" sufferers receive than being selected as "the salt of the earth" and "the light of the world," preaching the true Catholic Faith during these most trying times. Remember, Our Lord promised that He and His Church would triumph. He always keeps His promises. Our Lord is giving us "Being Old" Catholics the opportunity to help Him in fulfilling this plan while we still have life on this planet and can still earn merit for ourselves and our deceased love ones, who may be suffering in Purgatory.

Lastly, considering the daunting task ahead, seeking assistance from those patron saints, known for their prowess in interceding for seemingly hopeless lost causes, would be a step in the right direction.

Saint Rita of Cascia, pray for us;
Saint Jude Thaddeus, pray for us;
Saint Philomena, pray for us;
Saint Gregory of Neocaesarea, pray for us.

Warning to "Being Old" sufferers: Take the devil seriously

The devil is the most powerful evil force that man will encounter in this mortal life. Like a predator on the prowl, the devil stocks his prey, engaging in what we call "a cat and mouse game," waiting for the right moment to trap an unsuspecting victim. Keep in mind that Old Scratch is well aware that you, the "Being Old" sufferer, are coming to the end of your life. He knows that you are potentially vulnerable—a prime candidate for his diabolical machinations in his quest to capture your soul. The predatory nature of this "cat and mouse game" has gone on throughout the course of history. The cat, the stronger of the two animals, relies on his strength in trying to capture the mouse. The mouse, on the other hand, relies on his whit to escape the clutches of his more powerful adversary. Because animals are not rational creatures, their lives and any pain afflicted upon them terminate at the point of death. Humans, who are stalked by the devil, differ in this regard. We have immortal spiritual souls. This means that our existence is never ending. Hence, this ongoing "cat and mouse game" between mankind and Old Scratch is serious business, which should not be taken lightly. It is paramount that, in our twilight years, we keep our eye on our final end, eternal happiness. Our suffering is a gift, a means to a glorious end. Hear Saint Paul:

> For the Spirit himself giveth testimony to our spirit, that we are the sons of God. And if sons, heirs also; heirs indeed of God, and joint heirs with Christ: yet so, *if we suffer with him*, that we may be also glorified with him. For I reckon that the sufferings of this time are not worthy to be compared with the glory to come, that shall be revealed in us (Romans 8:16-18).

For those "Being Old" readers, who were brought up in the 1940s and 50s, you might recall the slapstick cartoon characters Tom (the cat) and Jerry (the mouse) who jousted and bantered with each other in a sometime violent fashion. Like most slapstick comedy at that time, however, there was no blood and gore or permanent loss of life or limb resulting from their encounters. In fact, there were times when Tom and Jerry worked together toward a common goal and behaved in a friendly manner.

Playing a "cat and mouse game" with Old Scratch should not be viewed in this light. It is not and never will be a light-hearted, friendly contest between two rivals who sometimes get together, sharing a common interest and enjoying each other's company. Rather, the game can end in frightening consequences for those cavalier and unsuspecting humans who treat it as such. Make no mistake about it! The devil is the cat and we are the mice. Old Scratch has no love for the human race. He hates God and His creatures, although like a slick politician, he will never openly say so. Yes, the Father of Lies is a ruthless competitor. He intends to be the winner of this cat versus mouse contest—no holds barred. His purpose is to capture your soul and drag you to Hell for eternity. Mankind's failure to take this diabolical game seriously clearly works toward Old Scratch's advantage. This is why Jesus Christ, His apostles, and the saints have repeatedly warned us about his real presence, the power that God allows him to possess over the tepid and ill-willed, and the nefarious tactics that he uses to lure those of good will to abandon the narrow road to life. Nevertheless, we must have confidence in Him Who has overcome the world and Satan. Too, we must bear in mind the words of Saint Paul, "And we know that to them that love God, all things work together unto good, to such as, according to his purpose, are called to be saints" (Romans 8:28).

Those of us who grew up in the Baby Boomer era were taught to fear the devil and to be vigilant in countering the temptations that he might concoct to lure us away from God into his clutches. While we knew that God was merciful, we were taught that He was all-just as well. If we failed to follow the teachings of His Church, our bodies and souls would be condemned to Hell for eternity—a most frightening prospect indeed. Back then this theme was preached from the pulpit. We were told firmly and forthrightly that the devil not only existed, but he was determined to destroy mankind. In order to constrain Old Scratch, a prayer to Saint Michael the Archangel was offered after every Low Latin Mass:

> Saint Michael the Archangel, defend us in battle, be our protection against the wickedness and snares of the devil, to you we humbly pray, by the divine power of God, cast into Hell all those evil spirits who prowl throughout the world seeking the ruin of souls.

This prayer reinforced the warning that the devil was to be feared. We needed to be on guard in protecting ourselves from him. We prayed to Saint Michael, asking him to provide us with this protection. Why Pope Paul VI in 1963 suppressed the Leonine Prayers, which included the prayer to Saint Michael, after Low Mass is a mystery to me and millions of the faithful.

During my youthful years, I, like many young people who lived through the turbulent 1960s, became caught up in the progressive movement of the times. I joined the Peace Corps, believing that dedicated men and women, with their combined efforts, could build a utopia right here on earth, "a civilization of love" we might say. President Lyndon Johnson's Great Society programs were put into action, and the Second Vatican Council promised a new springtime in the Catholic Church — an opening to the modern world and other religions. How exciting and engaging this seemed at the time. The Great Society and the changes in the Church filled us with optimism and confidence. We believed that mankind could accomplish anything if the human race diligently applied itself. God was not necessary, and the devil—he was nothing more than a Halloween character, a cloven-footed beast with a spiked tail, fire-breathing nostrils and two horns. Although he carried a pitchfork, this was only for decorative purposes—nothing to be feared.

As the 1960s progressed, we were euphoric, chanting that it was a time to move forward—a time to chuck Old Scratch into the dust bin of the past. In 1965, on the Feast of the Immaculate Conception, the Second Vatican Council was closed by Pope Paul VI. A new springtime was just over the horizon. Building the Great Society was on the march. Doing battle with the devil and his minions was not a part of this plan.

"The devil is dead" mantra became increasingly infectious throughout the 1960s. While much of the world was celebrating this new freedom from dark superstition, an "enlightenment" that delighted Lucifer "the one-time Light-Bearer," Paul Harvey, a legendary ABC radio commentator, delivered his famous "If I Were the Devil" speech on April 3, 1965. Harvey's speech was delivered before abortion and other perversions were legalized. It was a clear prophecy of that which was to come and is so blatantly evident today. Like George Orwell's *1984*, Harvey's radio message was a warning to all those who have eyes to see and ears to hear. This overlooked and ignored speech of the past is as follows:

> If I were the devil...I mean if I were the Prince of Darkness. I would of course, want

to engulf the whole earth in darkness. I would have a third of its real estate and four-fifths of its population, but would not be happy until I seized the ripest apple on the tree, so I could get about however necessary to take over the United States. I would begin with a campaign of whispers. With the wisdom of a serpent, I would whisper to you what I whispered to Eve. "Do as you please." "Do as you please." To the young, I would whisper, "The Bible is a myth." I would convince them that man created God instead of the other way around. I would confide that bad is good, and that what is good is "square." In the ears of the young marrieds, I would whisper that work is debasing and that cocktail parties are good for you. I would caution them not to be extreme in religion, in patriotism, in moral conduct. And the old, I would teach to pray. I would teach them to say after me: "Our Father, which art in Washington…"

If I were the devil, I'd educate authors in how to make lurid literature exciting so that anything else would appear dull and uninteresting. I'd threaten TV with dirtier movies and vice versa. And then, if I were the devil, I'd get organized. I'd infiltrate unions and urge more loafing and less work, because idle hands usually work for me. I'd peddle narcotics to whom I could. I'd sell alcohol to ladies and gentlemen of distinction. And I'd tranquilize the rest with pills. If I were the devil, I would encourage schools to refine young intellects but neglect to discipline emotions…let those run wild. I would designate an atheist to front for me before the highest courts in the land and I would get preachers to say "she's right." With flattery and promises of power, I could get the courts to rule to construe as against God and in favor of pornography, and thus, I would evict God from the courts, and then the school house, and then the houses of Congress and then, in His own churches. I would substitute psychology for religion, and I would deify science because in that way men and women would become smart enough to create super weapons but not wise enough to control them.

If I were the devil, I'd make the symbol of Easter an egg, and the symbol of Christmas a bottle. If I were the devil, I would take from those who have and I would give to those who wanted, until I had killed the incentive of the ambitious. And then, my police state would force everyone back to work. Then, I could separate families, putting children in uniform, women in coal mines, and objectors in slave camps. In other words, if I were Satan, I'd just keep doing what he is doing.

Paul Harvey, good day.

Warnings about the devil, such as Paul Harvey's, fell on deaf ears. Spurred on by our sense of being freed from the seemingly superstitious fears of the past and fueled with youthful exuberance, we broke the old rules in our quest to build a paradise on earth. It was in the 1960s, at the time when Harvey delivered his speech, that our break with those generations preceding us began to emerge. Smoking pot became "no big deal." Experimentation with both legal and illegal drugs started to become commonplace. Cohabitation was touted as the alternative to marriage. Promiscuity became a virtue and virginity was ridiculed. Civil disobedience and violence sprung up on college campuses and spread into a number of cities across the country. The "You can't trust anyone over thirty" mantra was drummed into the heads of youthful rebels who arrogantly believed that they knew more than their parents, grandparents, and persons in positions of authority. Crude and obscene behavior became increasingly more acceptable and self-indulgence was encouraged — "If it feels good, do it," we were told.

As we moved into the 1970s, the seeds of rebellion, which were sown in the preceding decade, led to the most diabolical piece of legislation in the history of our country. On January 22, 1973, the Supreme Court, in *Roe v. Wade*, declared that women had a fundamental right to abortion guaranteed under the United States Constitution. This has led to the slaughter of well over fifty million infants in the last four decades. In 1965, I suspect that Paul Harvey delivered his "If I Were the Devil" speech as a warning of that which was to come eight years later. Despite the fact that the evidence is right before us, the secularists would continue to argue—"There is no devil here. He is an imaginary creature concocted by fanatical Christians, particularly the old Catholic Church whose purpose was to manipulate and control the ignorant laity. Get real. This is the twenty-first century." Satan laughed with glee as rock stars chimed in. They either implicitly denied the devil's existence, as in John Lennon's "Imagine" in which we are to imagine there's no heaven, hell, or religion, or they pleaded for his rehabilitation, like The Rolling Stones' "Sympathy for the Devil" album. Some groups, whose names warrant no mention, even advocated his worship.

The "If I Were the Devil" speech drew some attention to the Prince of Darkness and his diabolical plan. To quote Harvey, the purpose of his plan was to destroy our nation—"to take over the United States," which Satan viewed as, "the ripest apple on the tree." Obviously, Harvey's speech alone lacked the necessary "fire power" to thwart the Prince of Darkness in the execution of his diabolical machinations. What Harvey needed was the support of secular and religious organizations, especially the Catholic Church founded by Our Lord, to check Satan in destroying our country, "the ripest apple" of all the nations on earth.

Why the Catholic Church one might ask? The answer is simple. Throughout the course of human history, it was the Catholic Church and the Catholic Church only, which had the spiritual muscle to keep Satan's legions at bay. It was the Catholic Church that led the charge in rousting out the devil and waging war on him and those "fellow travelers" who supported his agenda. This is why it was called the Church Militant. The prayer to Saint Michael, the Index of Forbidden Books, and the Legion of Decency were just some of the weaponry employed to keep Old Scratch in check. As we entered the decade of the 1960s, the Church Militant continued to be a powerful force, repeatedly exposing and thwarting the Prince of Darkness's diabolical plans. However, in 1965, the Second Vatican Council came to an end. The Church Militant was about to change. Triumphalism would be verboten.

Focusing on the devil and the "cat and mouse game" tactics that he uses to lure us into Hell was put on the back burner (no pun intended). Social justice, dialoguing with other religions, and performing good works were now emphasized. The results of these changes, no matter how well intentioned, soon led to disastrous consequences: thousands of priests and nuns abandoned their vocations; Catholic schools and seminaries were closed; Mass attendance decreased sharply; annulments rose significantly; a vast majority of Catholics stopped believing in the Real Presence; sex education in Catholic schools was pushed by our own bishops; and, as noted earlier, sex scandals and their cover-up reached an all-time high. Ignoring the devil and the failure to recognize his great power gave him a free reign to pursue his evil agenda. The rapid moral decline both in and outside of the Church would certainly support this thesis.

Even Pope Paul VI, the champion of the Second Vatican Council, acknowledged that the devil was at the root of the escalating moral decay. In a homily dated June 29, 1972, only seven years after the closing of the Second Vatican Council and Paul Harvey's speech, Pope Paul uttered the following lamentation:

> We believed that after the Council would come a day of sunshine in the history of the Church. But instead there came a day of clouds and storms, and of darkness...And how did this come about? We will confide to you the thought that maybe, we ourselves admit in free discussion, that may be unfounded, that there has been a power, an adversary power. Let us call him by his name: the devil. It is as if some mysterious, no, it is not mysterious, from some crack the smoke of Satan has entered the temple of God.

As the reader can see, acknowledging that the devil—"the smoke of Satan"—was the catalyst, who orchestrated the "clouds" and "storms" and the "darkness" undermining the Council, must have been difficult for Pope Paul. He was one of the key architects introducing the changes in the Church. Like many of his cohorts at that time, he failed to give the devil his due. Yet, the pope on this day June 29, 1972, called a spade a spade. He affirmed the devil's existence and his great power in influencing human affairs. This took some courage given the fact that the pope was surrounded by a sea of modernists.

Of course Pope Paul's quote raised a firestorm of criticism, from those who disagreed with his contention that "Satan had entered the temple of God." Some questioned the authenticity of the quote claiming it was taken out of context, misinterpreted, translated inaccurately, or that it simply did not exist. Others argued Pope Paul was referring only to those priests and bishops who ignored liturgical guidelines and were irreverent in following the rubrics of the new Mass. According to these critics, the Pope believed these culprits were puffed up with their own pride and vanity, personality traits attributed to the devil. In other words, it was not Satan, an individual spiritual person, influencing their thoughts and subsequent behavior. Rather, it was their mental and emotional state that contributed to the problems plaguing the Church.

More than four decades have passed since Pope Paul called out the devil by his name, claiming that "the smoke of Satan had entered the temple of God." Despite this, nothing has changed. The Prince of Darkness continues to prowl about among us. Like the elephant in the room, he remains unidentified, ignored, and unfettered, preaching his diabolical gospel to those who are hell-bent on constructing the City of Man. Meanwhile the murder of infants and the sale of their body parts; homosexual "marriage"; the abuse of drugs and alcohol; unjust, never ending wars waged for political and financial gain; and an intrusive government that "spins" the truth rather than seek justice marches on as though "all is well with the world."

In light of the preceding, we "Being Old" sufferers need to mobilize our spiritual resources to make sure that we do not fall victim to Old Scratch's evil manipulations. Acknowledging his existence and taking his great power seriously are the first steps toward reaching this goal. Because we are in the process of decline, we are increasingly more vulnerable. Praying for the strength to ward off Satan's assaults should, therefore, be our number one priority in our godless society, which has become so morally dulled that even commonsense is no longer common. Let's begin with the first step: "Saint Michael the Archangel…"

Be prepared: Thinking as Our Lord intended will be challenging

"He that is not with me is against me," spoken by Our Lord in the Gospel of Saint Matthew, chapter 12, verse 30, is a hard saying. It shows that Our Blessed Lord drew a clear line in the sand between Himself and His enemies. He intentionally polarized the world, placing its inhabitants into one of two camps. People were either with Him and His Church or they were against Him. He refused to let them take a middle-of-the-road position. Claiming that they were neutral was unacceptable. In fact, throughout the Gospels, Christ engaged in what modern man calls "black-and-white" thinking. He described the world as consisting of two principalities, good vs. evil. These principalities were to be at constant war with each other—an ongoing battle between Our Lord and the Prince of the World for the souls of men until the end of time. Christ insisted that we take sides in this battle. Our Lord specifically condemned these so-called moderates in the Book of Revelations:

> I know your works: you are neither hot nor cold. Would you were hot or cold! So, because you are lukewarm, and neither hot

nor cold, I will spew (vomit) you out of my mouth (3:15-16).

So much for those middle-of-the-road pundits, whose goal is to appease others and compromise His truth. Hence, the Church Militant was formed. Our Lord expected that all mankind should become members of the Church He founded, if they wished to save their souls. No other choice was acceptable.

Today's modernists would find the preceding to be disturbing. As noted earlier, they would accuse Christ of being too black and white in His thinking. They would further insist that the truth is still evolving and what constitutes truth today will change with the times. There are no absolutes. In light of this, the dogma that "outside the Catholic Church there is no salvation" would be viewed as absurd. Modern thinkers would argue that subjectivity is in, and dogmas proclaiming to be absolutely true would be out, in this more enlightened era.

Catholics, like Christ, must draw a line in the sand. When it comes to the Catholic Church, there is no compromise on matters of faith and morals. True Catholics contend that Christ the King is the absolute ruler of all mankind and He should be honored as such. The teachings of the "one, holy, catholic, and apostolic Church" — the four marks — are etched in stone and must be followed at the peril of losing one's soul. Christ instructed the clergy and laity to openly preach His truth "from the housetops." Therefore, it stands to reason that the Church hierarch, in particular, should respect and protect those who preach His Word and proclaim their loyalty to the Church He founded. However, this is hardly the case today. Rather, the opposite is true. Today's Catholics are reviled and mocked when they stand up without compromise for Christ and His infallible teachings on faith and morals. In some Middle Eastern countries and Nigeria and Sudan, Catholics and other Christians are being beheaded or hacked to death with machetes by the thousands for refusing to convert to Islam. So far, in the West, we are not yet being called to martyrdom. Not yet. In China, thousands of Catholics have died or are still being held in prisons or slave labor camps. (See the Cardinal Kung Foundation website at cardinalkungfoundation.org for information on the ongoing persecution of the Church in China.)

What does this mean for those "Being Old" Catholics, who are trying to practice their Faith in a world that is becoming increasingly more hostile to the Catholic Church and its teachings? First and foremost, we must recognize that forming close relationships in the secular world can be most difficult indeed. Although secularists can be affable on the surface, they may have strong underlying feelings of hostility about the Church Militant, blaming it for all of the ills of the past. If you are a traditional Catholic, you might be viewed as a representative of the old Church, which can evoke these feelings. This negative prejudice can quickly be applied to you, particularly if you are a vocal advocate and defender of the Catholic Faith. Being an old and suffering Catholic can be extremely stressful. The last thing that we want is to have strained relationships with family and friends when our demise might be close at hand. It is at this time that human compassion and support are needed. However, if you think and act as Christ intended, this may be denied to you. Old Scratch will be working overtime, tempting you "to go along to get along." Pray for the strength to endure, especially when you are feeling most vulnerable and alone. Christ promised that you will receive a great reward in Heaven for doing so.

Keep in mind that if you are a traditional Catholic, your relationships with Novus Ordo Catholic family and friends can be problematic, especially with those who have drifted away from the Church and no longer practice the Faith. Those "Being Old" Catholics of your generation might recognize and oppose the false teachings and novelties that followed the Second Vatican Council. However, they may have chosen "to go along to get along" rather than cause turmoil and conflict with the parish priest and those most dear to them. Traditional Catholics are likely to prick the conscience of family and friends who should know better. Again, this can quickly arouse feelings of guilt and anger, which can be projected on to you, the traditional Catholic. You will be blamed for creating emotional upheaval by those who disagree with you. Because they are spiritually blind, they will fail to recognize and reconcile this problem. Rather, you are likely to be the recipient of their heated condemnation.

Being disrespected can be painful, especially when it comes from those with whom we once formed close relationships. Fruitful past relationships are built on trust—the belief that our real friends not only understand, but would advocate for us when others engage in gossip, disparaging our commitment to traditional Catholic teachings. Unfortunately, this may not be the case. Rather in private conversations, those whom you once trusted might openly agree with your critics. Even if they say nothing, however, their silence can be interpreted as giving tacit approval to your more vocal adversaries' contentions. Refusing to take sides provides you, the traditional Catholic, with no solace. In fact, you are likely to feel betrayed if you have placed your trust in a person who fails to support you when you are surrounded by jackals attacking the Faith and your commitment to it. Friends who sit on the fence are not friends. Their neutrality actually strengthens those who are against and even hate the Church Militant.

True friendships are hard to come by unless that person shares your beliefs. Traditional Catholics must be steeled to the fact that they are at war with the Prince of the World and his earthly trappings. Christ clearly identified the enemy and insisted that we align ourselves with Him in this battle. Christ sanctioned no "gray" areas, nor "safe zones," that can be used as excuses to proclaim neutrality or as asylums to hide from reality. Like it or not, we must choose to either serve Him or mammon. There is no middle ground. Cleverly formulated rationalizations concocted by even the most intelligent men will never be able to reconcile the differences between them.

Such efforts will always be in vain. We are either with Him or against Him.

As traditional Catholics, we must accept the fact that we might be vilified if we think as Christ demands. Aligning ourselves with Him places us against Satan, the world, and those family and friends who are willing to compromise His Church and its teachings. "He who is not with me is against me" is not an artificial distinction created by Christ to stir up controversy. Rather, it is a true depiction of reality, with which we must cope for the rest of our lives.

God give us "Being Old" sufferers the grace to not fall prey to human respect in these our final days here on earth. Give us the strength to set good example and to advocate for Your Church in these so-called enlightened times.

Reinstating the Holy Rosary and devotions to Our Blessed Mother

In the previous chapter on unanswered prayers, I mentioned that I was a baseball enthusiast in my youthful years. I cited a time when I was competing for the batting championship. The night before an important game, I said three Rosaries. I petitioned Our Blessed Mother—Our Lady of the Rosary—for the number of hits that I would need to win this cherished title. Lo and behold! I had a perfect day at the plate, three hits in three at bats. I was fourteen years old at the time—the year was 1953.

In the 1940s and 50s, praying to Our Blessed Mother was a common practice. Catholic families prayed the Rosary daily; processions honoring Our Lady were important events; the months of October and May were dedicated to Our Heavenly Mother; and short but powerful prayers such as "O Mary, conceived without sin, pray for us who have recourse to thee" were uttered with frequency when asking Our Lady for assistance.

We were taught that Our Blessed Mother appeared to Saint Dominic in the year 1214. She was carrying beads and instructed Saint Dominic on how to say the Rosary. Our Lady promised that "Whatever you ask in the Rosary will be granted."

This Marian apparition received the title Our Lady of the Rosary. Saint Dominic preached and instructed others as Our Blessed Mother requested, and a great number of conversions took place.

As the years passed, the practice of saying the Rosary diminished. In order to reinstate the importance of this prayer, Our Lord Jesus appeared to Blessed Alan de la Roche in the fifteenth century and stated the following:

> You are crucifying Me again and because you have all the learning and understanding that you need to preach My Mother's Rosary, and you are not doing so. If you only do this, you could teach many souls the right path and lead them away from sin…

Needless to say, Blessed Alan honored Our Lord's request, and once again great numbers of people converted to the Catholic Faith. Shortly after Our Lord's apparition, Our Lady appeared to Blessed Alan and made the following fifteen promises to those who recite the Holy Rosary:

> "Whoever shall faithfully serve me by the recitation of the Rosary, shall receive signal graces."

> "I promise my special protection and the greatest graces to all those who shall recite the Rosary."

> "The Rosary shall be a powerful armor against Hell; it will destroy vice, decrease sin, and defeat heresies."

"The Rosary will cause virtue and good works to flourish; it will obtain for souls the abundant mercy of God; it will withdraw the hearts of men from the love of the world and its vanities, and it will lift them to the desire of eternal things. Oh, that souls will sanctify themselves by this means."

"The soul, which recommends itself to me by the recitation of the Rosary, shall not perish."

"Whoever shall recite the Rosary devoutly, applying himself to the consideration of its sacred mysteries shall never be conquered by misfortune. God will not chastise him in His justice, he shall not perish by an unprovided death; if he be just he shall remain in the grace of God, and become worthy of eternal life."

"Whoever shall have a true devotion of the Rosary shall not die without the sacraments of the Church."

"Those who are faithful to recite the Rosary shall have during their life and at their death the light of God and the plenitude of His graces; at the moment of death they shall participate in the merits of the saints in paradise."

"I shall deliver from Purgatory those who have been devoted to the Rosary."

"The faithful children of the Rosary shall merit a high degree of glory in Heaven."

"You shall obtain all you ask of me by the recitation of the Rosary."

"All those who propagate the Holy Rosary shall be aided by me in their necessities."

"I have obtained from my Divine Son that all the advocates of the Rosary shall have for intercessors the entire celestial court during their life and at the hour of death."

"All who recite the Rosary are my sons and daughters, and brothers and sisters of my only Son Jesus Christ."

"Devotion of my Rosary is a great sign of predestination."

By the time of Blessed Alan's death in 1475, the Rosary was a firmly established form of prayer in the Catholic Church and has continued to be so for the past five hundred years. Its importance was summed up by Our Lady, "Every Rosary you recite with me has the effect of restricting the action of the Evil One, of drawing away souls from his pernicious influence."

As the preceding indicates, praying the Rosary and devotions to Our Blessed Mother were high profile, important events for those of us who were reared in the Catholic Church in the 1940s and 50s — the "Being Old" generation. What is most striking to me, when I reflect back on those years, is how much influence the Catholic Church had on the secular world before the closing of the Second Vatican

Council. Consider Hollywood, for example, and the movies that were made at that time. In 1943 *The Song of Bernadette* starring Jennifer Jones, Charles Bickford, Vincent Price, and Lee J. Cobb was a box office hit. *The Miracle of Our Lady of Fatima* was released in 1952. The cast consisted of Sammy Ogg as Francisco Marto, Sherry Jackson as Jacinta Marto, and Susan Witney as Lucia Santos. The Catholic Church and Our Blessed Mother were treated with reverence back in those "Being Old" days gone by.

Let's fast forward to the year 1972 — twenty-nine years after *The Song of Bernadette* was released — twenty years after the release of *The Miracle of Our Lady of Fatima* and seven years after the closing of the Second Vatican Council. Within that short time, the praying of the Rosary and honoring Our Lady not only diminished, but Our Lady has been treated contemptuously as well. The beginning of these insults occurred during the 1972-73 football season. It was at this time that two seemingly innocuous, but nevertheless sacrilegious puns were directed toward Our Blessed Mother, the heart of the Holy Family. These commonly used little insults were called the "Immaculate Reception" and the "Hail Mary pass."

The term "Immaculate Reception" was coined following a divisional playoff game between the Pittsburg Steelers and the Oakland Raiders on December 23, 1972. With twenty-two seconds left, the Raiders were ahead by a single point. Franco Harris caught a game-winning touchdown pass that bounced off another player just before the ball was about to hit the ground. This "miraculous" ending led to the infamous moniker called the "Immaculate Reception," a play on the "Immaculate Conception," the dogma proclaiming that the Blessed Virgin Mary, the Mother of Jesus Christ and the Son of God, was conceived without original sin.

The Immaculate Reception moniker was first used publicly by Myron Cope, a Pittsburg sportscaster. He thought that changing Conception to Reception was not only clever but humorous as well. However, Cope was initially hesitant about using this on his show. Perhaps he was concerned how the Church Militant would respond to what could be interpreted as an insult to this sacred dogma? After all, it wasn't so long ago that the Church would have not only voiced abhorrence to such an insult, but would have demanded a public apology for such brazen behavior. The Catholic Church had moral authority back then, and mocking its dogmas could lead to serious repercussions. But this was 1972. A change in the Church's ecumenical thinking was now in full swing. Cope might have recognized that the once Church Militant had now softened and was more concerned with embracing the world rather than standing forthrightly against those evils, which were corrupting it. Whatever his thoughts might have been, Cope decided to take a chance. He used the term "Immaculate Reception" on his television show. It was not only well received, but has endured to this day. In fact, a statue of Franco Harris catching the "Immaculate Reception" pass is in the Pittsburg International Airport for all to see.

In our upside-down world, many would consider the changing of the Immaculate Conception to the Immaculate Reception as a harmless little joke. They would argue that poking a little fun at the Church and its dogmas is nothing to get alarmed over. Good sports recognize this and know how to "go along to get along," rather than overreact to a little Catholic ribbing. The secularists would insist that people shouldn't take their religion too seriously if they want to get along with others. After all, that is what being ecumenical is all about.

But there is another dimension to be considered here. Would Jesus Christ consider the "Immaculate Reception" to be a harmless little joke? On the contrary, the Son of God most likely would consider this to be an insult to His Mother, who was conceived without original sin and brought Him into the world to save mankind. Over the centuries, Christ has repeatedly sent His Mother into this world, warning mankind about the chastisements that would be inflicted upon us if we failed to follow His Laws. Does this sound like a God who would "laugh off" irreverent wordplay about the Immaculate Conception and the Virgin birth? How would Our Lord react to those who participate in this unholy charade, especially those of us who have been reared in the Catholic Faith and should know better? So offended was Our Lord in regard to the outrages committed against His Mother that, in 1930, He named five of them specifically to Sister Lucia of Fatima, and the first of these was the blasphemy against the Immaculate Conception.

Yes! The Immaculate Reception entered the world unscathed and even heralded by football enthusiasts across the country. It not only became a part of American football folklore, but it opened up the floodgates that would be directed toward Our Lady. Three years after the Immaculate Reception, on December 28, 1975, another playoff game took place between the Dallas Cowboys and the Minnesota Vikings. The Vikings were leading the Cowboys with only twenty-four seconds remaining. The Cowboys had the ball at midfield. Roger Staubach, the Cowboys quarterback, threw a fifty-yard pass that was caught for the winning touchdown. Staubach was interviewed following the game. He was quoted as saying, "I got knocked down on the play…I closed my eyes and said a Hail Mary."

Staubach, who is a practicing Catholic, meant no disrespect when he made this comment. In fact, he was probably earnest in seeking Our Lady's assistance in his quest for this victory. However, it is unlikely that the secular press would have viewed it in this light. To them, the Hail Mary became the new moniker for every desperation pass thrown in the last few seconds of a football game, in which the odds of winning were very small indeed. It is unlikely they would have considered that the Hail Mary is a most revered prayer, the first part given by God Himself. Rather, the Hail Mary pass became the newly coined phrase to replace the "alley-oop" and the "long bomb" as the last-ditch effort to win a football game. Like the Immaculate Reception, there were no complaints about the light-hearted way in which the Hail Mary was treated. The term caught on and continues to be used today.

To add insult to injury, the greatest Hail Mary pass that was ever thrown occurred on November 23, 1984. Boston College, a Catholic institution, played the University of Miami on this day. Boston College was losing the game with only six seconds remaining. Doug Flutie, Boston College's quarterback, threw a forty-eight yard desperation pass toward the end zone, which was caught for the winning touchdown. Again, the Hail Mary pass moniker was paraded out in full force in describing the play. In fact, Boston College commissioned the construction of a statue of Doug Flutie, who is a Catholic, commemorating his throwing of the pass that led to their victory. On the base of this statue, there is a sign referring to the Hail Mary pass in quotes. This statue is proudly displayed on the campus today. The Hail Mary moniker had become quite common since the Dallas Cowboys' victory over the Minnesota Vikings nine years earlier. As a result, no one seems concerned that treating the Angelic Salutation in this fashion could be viewed as sacrilegious to those both inside and outside the Catholic Church.

Keep the following in mind. Blasphemous language is sacrilegious. It shows contempt for God and His Church, thereby depriving Them of the sacredness to which They are entitled. The Hail Mary, which is an integral part of the Catholic Church's Holy Tradition, is as follows: "Hail Mary, full of grace! The Lord is with Thee; blessed are thou among women and blessed is the fruit of thy womb, Jesus.

Holy Mary, Mother of God, pray for us sinners, now and at the hour of our death. Amen." Think about these hallowed words and how they have now become associated with a forward pass, once called a "long bomb" by the secular media.

In light of the preceding, we "Being Old" sufferers, by our example, need to honor Our Blessed Mother. Remember, Our Lord asked us to act like "the salt of the earth" and "the light of the world." He would expect us, therefore, to defend Our Lady and to treat her with the devotion and respect to which she is entitled. Reinstating the Rosary as an integral part of our prayer life, if we have not already done so, is an important first step in this regard. As noted in the fifteen promises revealed by Our Lady to Blessed Alan de la Roche, saying the daily Rosary can earn merit for us and family and friends who are suffering in Purgatory. Moreover, keep in mind that Our Blessed Mother also promised Francisco, Jacinta, and Lucia—the three seers of Fatima—great graces for those who observed the First Saturday for five consecutive months in honor of her Immaculate Heart. Our Lady's promise was as follows:

> I promise to help at the hour of death, with the graces needed for salvation, whoever on the First Saturday of five consecutive months shall:
>
> (1) confess and receive Holy Communion;
>
> (2) recite five decades of the Rosary;

(3) and keep me company for fifteen minutes while meditating on the fifteen mysteries of the Rosary, with the intention of making reparation to Me.

Five Joyful Mysteries: The Annunciation; The Visitation; The Nativity; The Presentation; Finding in the Temple.

Five Sorrowful Mysteries: Agony in the Garden; Scourging at the Pillar; Crowning with the Thorns; Carrying the Cross; The Crucifixion.

Five Glorious Mysteries: The Resurrection; The Ascension; The Descent of the Holy Ghost; The Assumption of the Blessed Virgin Mary; The Coronation of the Blessed Virgin Mary.

Our Blessed Mother has made a treasure trove of graces available to those who faithfully pray the Rosary and honor her requests. She has been designated by Our Lord, Jesus Christ, to be the Mediatrix of All Graces. In other words, all graces and blessings that are given to us by Our Lord come through her. Let all Catholics, particularly those of us in the "Being Old" stage of life whose time to earn merit for ourselves and our loved ones will soon end, take full advantage of Our Lady's benevolence and generosity. Most humbly we ask: "O Mary, conceived without sin, pray for us who have recourse to thee."

A spiritual war of words

Over the past fifty years, our society has become so morally and spiritually dulled that even those "Being Old" Catholics, who were reared before Vatican II, fail to recognize the mounting corruption infecting us. An honest examination of our conscience and frequent Confession are essential in preventing us from sinking further and further into the sin of presumption. However, because we now overrate our "goodness," believing that we are better than we really are, Confession is no longer taken seriously. The once long lines of those waiting to confess their sins have significantly diminished. It is not unusual to find fellow "Being Old" Catholics of my generation who have not been to Confession for decades. Old Scratch is having a field day, harvesting the souls of a presumptuous laity, who have come to believe that Our Lord is so merciful He will send us all to Heaven, despite our violation of His Laws and His insistence that we obey them.

Presumptuous Catholics might be compared to the proverbial frog placed in a pot of cold water on a stove. The poor creature fails to recognize that he is going to be boiled alive. Because the progression leading to his demise is gradual, the unsuspecting frog basks in the cool water, adjusting to the slowly rising temperature. By the time the water hits the boiling point, it is too late for the frog to save himself.

For those of us who are in the "Being Old" stage of life, in which we are becoming increasingly more vulnerable, mobilizing our spiritual resources so that we do not share the frog's fate is of the utmost importance. Keep in mind that the man who fails to recognize the seriousness of mortal sins and has no plan for combating them will become grist for Old Scratch's mill. Unlike the frog, we have an immortal soul which, if left unprotected, can become easily corrupted. Those who are spiritually lackadaisical are prime targets for the Father of Lies. His temptations, leading to sinful transactions, will appear to be harmless. He will fill your mind with carefully crafted words and slogans such as "it's no big deal" and "everybody does it," the purpose of which is to lull you into a spiritual stupor.

As a clinical psychologist, I have increasingly come to appreciate the importance of words and how these influence our emotions and the choices that we make. What we say to ourselves, the actual words, phrases, and sentences, have a major impact on what we feel and how we act. The devil, who is an expert in manipulating our fallen nature, crafts his language accordingly. Old Scratch knows our weaknesses. He uses words, which are designed to exploit our particular vulnerabilities and lure us into doing his bidding.

In the days before the Second Vatican Council, the warring good and evil principalities, competing for the souls of mankind, were clearly identified and the battle between them was openly discussed and taken seriously. For example, we were taught that two spiritual beings stood on each of our shoulders — the devil was on the left and our Guardian Angel was on the right. Each had access to one of our corresponding ears. The devil was forever whispering into our left ear, prodding us to follow the ways of the world and encouraging us to engage in sinful behavior. Our Guardian Angel, on the other hand, would whisper into our right ear, stressing the importance of following God's laws and avoiding the trap that Old Scratch was setting for us. These back and forth battles involved verbal fisticuffs, actual debates between these warring spiritual entities, one promoting evil and the other advocating good. It was up to us to distinguish between substance and sophistry and to choose wisely. Our Guardian Angel and the message that he conveyed were taken seriously and we were encouraged to listen carefully to what he had to say.

> Behold I will send my angel, who shall go before thee, and keep thee in thy journey, and bring thee into the place that I have prepared. Take notice of him, and hear his voice, *and do not think him one to be contemned:* for he will not forgive when thou hast sinned, and my name is in him. But if thou wilt hear his voice, and do all that I speak, I will be an enemy to thy enemies, and will afflict them that afflict thee. And my angel shall go before thee… (Exodus 23:20-24, italics mine).

In light of the preceding, it makes sense that being more aware of this internally based spiritual warfare, the war between good and evil, and acquiring the ability to monitor and control its outcome would be most important to the salvation of our soul. In order to achieve this goal, two tasks need to be mastered: First, we must learn to identify those thoughts that fan the fires of temptation and make it appear to be so attractive; and second, we need to formulate counter-thoughts to combat and replace these so that we do not fall prey to Old Scratch's lure. These counter-thoughts would consist of Catholic language, actual words, phrases, and sentences, based on our Faith and how it should be lived and put into practice.

The following is an example of how the preceding model works. Let's imagine that you and your spouse are retired. You are both in the "Being Old" stage of life. You have contracted several health problems, which have been plaguing you for more than a year. You follow your doctor's instructions, eat moderately, exercise three times a week, and have no bad habits. Unfortunately, your health has not improved. Despite your best efforts, you feel stuck in a seemingly unending cycle of pain and discomfort. Prior to your current maladies, you were athletic and able to engage in vigorous exercise. Playing eighteen holes of golf was "a piece of cake." You were also able to play a full-court game of basketball with players twenty years younger than you. You received numerous compliments lauding your strength and stamina. Younger men affectionately looked up to you, calling you "the old man." They often told you that they hope to be like you when they reach their retirement years.

You used to take your good health for granted. Now that it seems to be slipping away, however, you have become increasingly anxious, fearing your life will never be the same and might even worsen. You have always been a practicing Catholic. Over the past few months, you have increased your prayers and have been attending daily Mass. You have prayed fervently, begging Our Lord to take this cross off of your shoulders and restore you to good health. So far no changes have occurred, and at times, you feel worse. Needless to say, you no longer can play eighteen holes of golf, and playing basketball is out of the question. To compound your health problems, you are having financial difficulties as well. Your wife has been working part-time to supplement your income. Added health bills have only exacerbated an already difficult situation.

You and your wife have recently been socializing with another "Being Old" couple in your retirement community. Joe, the husband, like you, has always been in good health and continues to be so. He is an excellent golfer and recently ran in a road race, placing first in his age group. Joe is a self-confident man who brags a bit about his athletic ability and accomplishments. In one of your discussions with Joe, he claimed that being old was a matter of perception. He contended that "you are as young as you feel" and "mind over matter" is at the root of curing most physical and mental health problems. Joe was a CEO of a major company. He retired with what he called "a golden parachute." Joe spends his money freely. He often talks about the five-star restaurants he frequents, and the lavish vacations that he and his wife have taken since he retired. Living well is obviously very important to Joe. Like you, Joe is a Catholic. However, he no longer regularly attends church. He is what you would call "a cafeteria Catholic," picking and choosing what he wants to believe. Joe drinks to excess on occasion and smokes expensive cigars. Needless to say, you find his cocky attitude annoying to say the least.

It is the annoyance—the irritation that you feel toward Joe, which needs to be focused upon in the preceding example. The irritation is the seed, planted by Old Scratch, which can serve as the catalyst to tempt you to engage in sinful thoughts, leading to envy, anger, and eventual despair. Your thought process might be as follows. You begin by telling yourself that you unfairly drew "the short straw" at this time of your life. Following this expression of your dissatisfaction, you tell yourself that these are supposed to be the "golden years," a time to enjoy life. You then continue with thoughts such as the following: "I have always been healthy, and now for no apparent reason my health has deteriorated. I followed my doctor's advice and I don't smoke, drink, or have poor habits. My suffering makes no sense. I worked for nearly forty years, saved my money, and lived frugally. I don't deserve this."

You were already anxious before Joe came into your life. His bravado has added to the stress that you are experiencing. Your mounting dislike for Joe, on top of your current health and financial difficulties, could become "the straw that broke the camel's back," if you fail to stop and control your errant thinking. Old Scratch is waiting in the wings, hoping to capitalize on your increasing anger directed toward the man with "the golden parachute."

As you can see, your antagonistic feelings toward Joe, fueled by your negative thinking, have set the stage for Old Scratch to tempt you. The following thoughts will then be crafted and nurtured by Old Scratch in order to encourage you to do his bidding: (1) "That jerk! He thinks he is so great. I would give anything to be healthy again. I would beat his brains out on the basketball court." (2) "He is always bragging about the trips that he takes and the fancy restaurants he goes to. I wish that he would choke on the food he eats there." (3) "This guy drinks, smokes, and abuses his body. Me, I take care of myself and I get sick. What a rip off! He is the one who deserves to be ill, not me." (4) "I don't get it! I pray and go to Mass and am still suffering. He mocks God and remains healthy. Where is God when I need Him? Praying is a waste of time." (5) "I worked all my life and lived frugally. There was no 'golden parachute' for me. I saved my money and lived 'by the rules.' Now with my current health problems, I'm having difficulty making ends meet. This is totally unfair." (6) "Joe is nothing but a bragging blowhard. I wish he would fall on his face and get what is coming to him. I hate him and what he stands for!"

Note that the preceding thoughts center on Joe and hoping that he would suffer and come to a bad ending in his life. By engaging in and willfully nurturing these angry thoughts we sin by envy, and despair could soon follow. These sins violate the laws of God, Who has commanded us to be charitable to one another. You can see that unless this sinful thinking is stopped and corrected, it could put the salvation of your soul in jeopardy.

Let's suppose you recognize that your thoughts are becoming destructive. You decide to stop these and then consciously attempt to replace them with the following counter-thoughts: "I am becoming increasingly more irritated with Joe. This is not doing me any good. I am getting envious because he is in a better financial position than me, even though I worked hard and lived frugally, which is what God would expect of me. Joe drinks too much and smokes, and yet he is still healthy. I am jealous of this too. Worst of all, I am becoming angry with God because He is not taking away my suffering—yet Our Lord suffered and died for our sins. How foolish I have been. Joe, with all his talents and earthly possessions, has lost his Faith. Pride is taking control of his life and is damning his soul. I should pity, not hate him."

Imagine how you would feel, if you were able to curb your self-destructive sinful thinking and replace this with counter-thoughts such as the preceding. The spiritual warfare within you would cease and you would experience inner peace. You would feel compassion for Joe, who is drowning in a sea of pride—the most deadly of all the Capital Sins that lead souls to Hell.

As you can see, the preceding scenario is an example of how Catholic thinking can be used to combat thoughts leading to the corruption and eventual destruction of your soul. Again, Catholic thinking consists of the actual words, phrases, and sentences that you might say to yourself when temptations such as envy, anger, and despair arise within you. It should be kept in mind that many temptations come from the devil. Remember how Old Scratch tempted Eve. Eve did not ask the devil to tempt her. Rather, he slyly planted thoughts of disobedience in her mind. The more Eve thought about disobeying God, the greater the temptation became. Her thoughts about eating the forbidden fruit and being like God intensified. Eve failed to stop and counter the sinful thoughts. As a result, they not only intensified but rapidly multiplied the more that she dwelt upon them. You know the rest of the story. Pride got the better of Eve and she did the devil's bidding.

An important point to keep in mind is that there are few of us who openly invite the devil to tempt us. Rather, like a thief in the night, he sneaks up on us, invading our minds with temptations, which appeal to our fallen human nature. These temptations are naturally attractive. Because our human nature is flawed and sin is so appealing, we often fail to see its danger. Instead of nipping sinful thinking in the bud, we, like Eve, dwell upon and nurture sinful thoughts until we are overcome by them. This is why Catholic thinking is so important. It can stop and replace sinful thoughts before they impair our relationship with God and lead us into Hell.

Needless to say, learning how to use Catholic language in order to combat sinful thinking, which comes from the Father of Lies, is not easy. Because it requires the use of our higher faculties, the mastering of our intellect and will, it lacks the attraction that the devil's temptations offer. Learning to use Catholic language demands that we examine our conscience, making an honest appraisal of what we are truly thinking, coupled with a sincere and persistent effort to put what we learn into practice. Above all, we must have a burning desire to follow God's plan. Using Catholic language is actually a form of prayer. It involves the application of Catholic principles and includes specific references to Holy Scripture, which can be of assistance in forming your thoughts as well.

In order to put the preceding into practice, the following steps need to be taken. First, as soon as you experience the temptation to sin, ask yourself this question: "What am I saying to myself that is leading me into temptation?" Second, try to write the actual words, which are occurring in your mind at that moment. Recording your thoughts will not only improve your self-insight, but it will help you to check and stop Sinful Thinking (ST) before the temptation worsens and you become overwhelmed. Once the ST has been identified, the third step would be to formulate Catholic Language (CL) that can be used to combat and replace ST. The actual writing of CL would be the best approach to use when you are first learning how to put this into practice. The more that you practice, the more skilled you will become in acquiring better thinking habits, which can be applied in coping with the Father of Lies and his false promises.

It should be kept in mind that writing your thoughts can be annoying, particularly when Old Scratch is tempting you. In fact, avoiding the writing of your thoughts will be a temptation. Old Scratch would prefer that you "chill out" and "go with the flow," especially when such thinking could lead you astray. He will appeal to the slothful side of your human nature, planting thoughts in your mind such as: "Having to go to this extreme (writing your thoughts) is silly and a waste of my time and effort. This is an assignment given to an elementary school child, not a mature adult like me." There are a number of excuses that Old Scratch will help you to concoct in order to weaken your resolve.

Writing your thoughts in a journal requires that you train your intellect and control your will. This leads to the acquisition of self-discipline, which is anathema to Old Scratch who wants you to become a prisoner of your senses. Like any difficult task, writing your thoughts and learning to control them will become easier with continued practice. Eventually, the writing and extra deliberation will not be necessary. Rather, the habit of using CL will be acquired and you will be able to "automatically" put this into practice as the need arises. Keep in mind that the habit of using CL can only be achieved with hard work and persistence. And remember, Old Scratch has no intention of helping you to make this task an easy one.

In the previous scenario, three mortal sins were identified. Joe was puffed up with the Capital Sin of pride and you were described as being envious and angry. Let's begin by examining Joe's pride and the subtle, unidentified thinking that stokes the hell fire of this grandfather of all Capital Sins. In Joe's case the sinful thoughts (ST) that might apply to him are as follows: "Because I am talented, intelligent, and athletic, I am better than other people. My superiority entitles me to special treatment. I am wealthy and deserve to be so. Being in a high social class is what counts in life. People who are poor are lazy and below me. They should be treated with contempt."

Obviously, if Joe's ST remain unchecked, the salvation of his soul would be in jeopardy. Stopping and replacing Joe's current ST with the following CL is offered: "We are all equal in the eyes of God. Those who are given talents will be expected to develop and use them in order to serve Him. They will be held accountable for failing to do so. God will be pleased if we use our gifts for the betterment of mankind. He will be displeased, however, if we boast or use these gifts to laud our superiority over others. Remember the Parable of Talents (Matthew 25:14-43). God was equally pleased with the servant who was given five talents, and doubled them, as with the servant who was given two talents, and did the same. God is concerned with my spiritual welfare. He abhors arrogance and prizes humility. Throughout Our Lord's life, He was charitable to others and humble. He mixed with both the wealthy, the poor, sinners, and the lepers and never preached that one social class was superior to the others. The fulfillment of His Laws is the standard by which He will judge me."

Now let's examine your irritation and the ST, which have mushroomed into anger and even hatred of Joe. The ST are as follows: "Life should be fair. I have the right to be healthy, and for no good reason, this has been taken away from me. My habits are good; I worked hard and I saved my money, living frugally. I practice my Faith and have been loyal to God and His Church. Joe ignores God and treats the Church with contempt. Instead of being punished, however, he gets rewarded. My golden years have turned into rust. The more that I think about this, the angrier I become. In fact, I'm furious. God! How I hate that man!"

Obviously, your fury if left unchecked could lead to the damnation of your soul. The following CL replacement for the ST is offered for your consideration: "The world is not a fair place. This is why God has promised us that we will be judged by Him. He, not the world, will give us perfect justice. All of us, no matter what, will be judged by the same standards. God commanded that we treat our enemies charitably. Saint Paul wrote: 'Do not avenge yourselves, beloved; for it is written, Vengeance is mine: I will repay, says the Lord. But if your enemy is hungry, give him food; if he is thirsty, give him drink; for by so doing, you will heap coals of fire upon his head. Be not overcome with evil but overcome evil with good' (Romans 12:19-21). I must leave justice to God and trust that He will fulfill His promise. If I treat my enemy charitably, I will be doing as Our Lord intended. Love for my neighbor, who just happens to be Joe, is what Our Lord expects from me. Wishing evil on Joe will not make me a better person. In fact, it is currently destroying me."

With regard to your envy, the following ST, which will need to be replaced with CL is as follows: "Look at all the good things that happen to Joe. He ignores God and no longer practices the Faith. He is healthy despite abusing alcohol and smoking. He has plenty of money. Look at me. I worked hard all of my life. Now because of unforeseen medical expenses, I am having financial difficulties. My wife has to work so that we can make ends meet. I wish I had Joe's good luck. If I had his money, I would be a happy person. I envy 'the golden parachute' that he received when he retired. He is free to do as he pleases. He lives 'the good life,' even though I don't think he deserves it."

The following CL replacement for your envious ST is offered: "Joe is fortunate that he is healthy, financially well off, and talented. However, the way that he is acting is not pleasing to Our Lord. This could lead to trouble in the future and the loss of his soul. Dwelling on Joe's good fortune is only making me resentful and envious. Christ commanded that I love my neighbor as myself. However, being envious is preventing me from living up to the minimum of this law. Christ warned us not to be envious of evil doers and their earthly possessions. Rather, we should behave charitably toward them. Being uncharitable in my sinful thinking is only increasing my frustration and worsening my envy. I need to stop and change this before it destroys me."

Interestingly, CL can be applied to all of the various sins leading to our spiritual destruction. For example, as mentioned throughout this book, the sin of presumption (a sin against the Holy Ghost) is quite prevalent today. A ST that would be attached to presumption would be as follows: "God is too merciful to send anyone to Hell. If Hell exists at all, nobody would be in it. God loves us too much to let this happen." To counter this presumptuous ST the following is offered: "It is true that God is all-merciful, but He is all-just as well. Our Lord promised that each and every iota of His Law must be fulfilled. He emphasized that we would be held accountable for even the smallest infractions. Christ specifically stated that Hell exists. Those who would not keep His Commandments while living, should they die unrepentant, would be sent there."

What about the sin of despair? If you are a "Being Old" practicing Catholic, who is praying to Our Lord for the relief of your suffering and your prayers appear to be unanswered, Old Scratch will fill your mind with sinful thoughts (ST) such as the following: "Prayers are a waste of time. You attend church and worship God and you get nothing in return. Can't you see that your situation is hopeless? Your suffering isn't going to improve. In fact, given your old age it is likely going to worsen. Then you will be more of a burden on your family and friends. They are probably already sick and tired of having to put up with you. Do yourself and those around you a favor. Take an overdose of pills and end it all. Not only will you finish suffering, but you won't be wasting your money on just staying alive for no good reason. You can at least then leave your family with an inheritance for which they will be grateful. Perhaps they could spend the money on a family vacation. They could reminisce about the good old days, celebrating your life when you were healthy and worth something. Take the pills and end the suffering! I know that you believe in God and fear Him. If there is a God and He is all-merciful, as you say He is, He will understand your plight and probably agree with me. Besides, how many times have you heard people say at the wake of the sufferer who just died, 'He is in a better place now.' The only difference between you and the previously deceased person is that this currently applies to you. Put an end to the continuation of this useless suffering before you end up like a blithering idiot and the object of everyone's pity."

We currently live in a society that touts euthanasia and physician-assisted suicide as panaceas for the ending of human suffering. These are wrapped in a cloak of "death with dignity," in order to make them appear to be not only acceptable, but noble as well. It would be easy to become a victim of the death with dignity slogan, a despair driven ST, of which Old Scratch is the author. In order to combat his cleverly worded ST, the following CL is offered: "Suicide is not an option. Yes. I am suffering now. But I know in my heart that Our Lord loves those of us who willingly accept this and offer it for the souls in Purgatory. Look at the lives of the great saints.

They were asked to suffer much more than me. Carrying Christ's cross with dignity sets the example that I wish to leave as a legacy to family and friends. If I pray and stay the course, Our Lord and Our Blessed Mother will not abandon me. This, they promised me, at the hour of my death. If I follow them, I will then truly be 'in a better place' when I die—Heaven not Hell. Hell is surely where I would go if I commit suicide."

In summation, the importance of words and their meaning can have a powerful influence on our emotions, the choices that we make, and how we behave. Old Scratch has concocted his own lexicon of carefully crafted words, phrases, and sentences, which are designed to encourage us to engage in worldly pursuits that run contrary to God's will. Old Scratch is an expert in exploiting our weaknesses. He is well aware of those vulnerabilities that plague "Being Old" Catholics and how to manipulate us into doing his bidding. The Father of Lies uses language to lull us into a spiritual stupor. Once this is achieved, he fills our minds with sinful thoughts. Old Scratch promises much. However, if we succumb to his verbal trickery, we will soon find out that these fall far short of our expectations.

In order to combat Old Scratch's plan, we need to learn to identify sinful thoughts (ST) and stop them before they overwhelm us. Using Catholic Language (CL), which is based on Catholic teachings and Holy Scripture to replace these dangerous ST, should then be put into practice. Keep in mind that Old Scratch's lexicon appeals to our lower nature. This is what makes temptations appear to be so attractive. Catholic Language (CL), which requires mastery of our intellect and will, lacks this attraction. Hard work and effort, therefore, will be necessary to acquire such mastery. As a result, Old Scratch will tempt you to avoid this task. Don't fall prey to the Father of Lies and his clever manipulations. It is clear, concise, and forthright Catholic thinking that needs to be developed and fostered in order to defeat Old Scratch and undo the stranglehold that he currently has on the world. It is up to us, "Being Old" Catholics, to set an example and to avoid becoming one of those spiritually-dulled persons who unwittingly follows Old Scratch into damnation. Keep in mind that we are at the end of life. This might be our last opportunity to change from the wide to the narrow road before our time runs out.

Epilogue

Throughout this book, I have attempted to focus on "Being Old" and the challenges that you will face in the final stage of life. It has been written from my perspective as a psychologist and traditional Catholic. As I have indicated, I was reared in the pre-conciliar Church, the teachings of which have been seared into my soul. After the closing of the Second Vatican Council, I floundered around in a sea of novelties, confusion, and disillusionment, until by the grace of God I rediscovered the Catholic Faith of my youth at the ripe old age of sixty. Although I was professionally active, I was on the cusp of "Being Old" and beginning to face the adversities discussed in these chronicles. I thank Our Lord every day for the grace that He bestowed upon me, leading me back to the Church of our fathers — the true Catholic Church with the Latin Mass and treasure trove of sacraments and prayers.

In light of the preceding, there is one final topic that needs to be addressed by those of us in the "Being Old" stage of life — facing our death, which will soon follow. It is important to keep in mind that no matter how much wealth we accumulate, no matter how famous we become, no matter how many friends we have made, and no matter how much professional success we have achieved, death puts a final end to all of these. Memories of the days gone by, awards we have won, and the class reunions we attended fade and become mere shadows of the past, eventually forgotten by the many generations that follow. These will count for little or nothing when we stand before God and receive His final judgment. Rather, Our Lord's evaluation on how we used the time allotted to us during our life here on earth will be all that matters. For any person who takes their Catholic Faith seriously, the thought of facing Our Lord on judgment day is a most frightening experience. Think about this. Our eternal happiness or damnation will hang in the balance. There will be no second chance or the opportunity to appeal our case to a higher authority. We will receive one or the other. How we have lived in God's eyes, not the eyes of our friends, family, or business associates, will count.

Again, thinking about the final judgment can be frightening. However, we must reflect upon this to insure that we do not become spiritually lax, like most others in our currently presumptuous "everybody goes to heaven" society. Because Jesus was kind, gentle, and merciful, we are quick to overlook that He is all-just and that He promised to hold us accountable for the least violation of His law. Jesus warned us that we should fear Him because He, and only He, has the power to condemn both our body and soul to Hell:

> Beware of the leaven of the Pharisees, which is hypocrisy. But there is nothing concealed that will not be disclosed, and nothing hid-

den that will not be made known. For what you have said in the darkness will be said in the light, and what you have whispered in the inner chambers will be preached on the housetops. But I say to you my friends, Do not be afraid of those who kill the body, and after that have nothing more than they can do. But I will show you whom to be afraid of; be afraid of him, who, after he has killed, has the power to cast into hell. Yes I say to you be afraid of him (Luke 12:1-5).

This quote from the Gospel of Saint Luke clearly indicates that Christ expects us to have a healthy fear of Him and His power to reward or punish us. While it is true that Jesus was gentle, kind, and merciful, He was not the "soft touch" that presumptuous persons make Him out to be. His words forthrightly indicate that He meant what He said. His final judgment of our soul will be a serious matter. Keep this in mind when Old Scratch tries to tempt you to give up your faith in Christ and His Church.

In order to prepare yourself to face the final judgment, consider the following. You will be on your own when this takes place. You will not have a team of clever lawyers, family members, or close friends who will be allowed to plead for the salvation of your soul. The absolute truth on how you lived your life will be disclosed to all interested parties involved with your case. "Who are the interested parties?" you might ask. They are as follows: first, Our Lord, Jesus Christ, Who will make the final Judgment; second, your Guardian Angel, who was assigned to protect you and provide for your spiritual welfare throughout the course of your life on earth; and third, Old Scratch who wants your soul to be condemned to the fires of Hell. These are the important litigants involved with your case. Imagine yourself appearing before this tribunal. Imagine waiting to be judged. What might you be thinking and feeling about that which is to come?

Think about what is to follow. Perhaps your Guardian Angel will be the first one called upon to plead your case. During his presentation, however, he might begin to pause, recalling the times that you ignored and failed to accept God's grace when it was offered to you. He may valiantly try to emphasize your meritorious actions, but will these be enough to offset your many violations of God's law?

Now imagine Old Scratch of Daniel Webster fame. He is lurking in the shadows, fervently waiting to make his case that your soul belongs to him. He noticed that your Guardian Angel was a bit anxious and balked somewhat in his attempt to save you. Although your Guardian Angel tried to cover-up his anxiety and appear to be confident, his body language indicated otherwise. This did not escape the clever and observant Old Scratch. He garnered strength from this observation. Now it is his turn to present his case. In a forceful tone of voice, Old Scratch pointed out the many times that you disregarded the teachings of Christ's Church. He proudly cited past blasphemies, sacrilegious Holy Communions, moments of debauchery, and sins of the flesh, which you freely committed. And what about the indecent jokes and the mockery of Church dogmas, which you so gleefully participated in even though you claimed to be a practicing Catholic?

Be on guard therefore. The scene depicted above is exaggerated deliberately. We must not be slack but, like Saint Paul instructs us, "work out [our] salvation with fear and trembling" (Phil. 2:12) and, at least in some way like him, "chastise [our] body and bring it under subjection" lest we "become a castaway" (1 Cor. 9:27). The devil is powerless to bring up sins that have been confessed with true contrition and firm purpose of amendment. Even God Himself, so to speak, has forgotten them. If we *persevere* in grace our Guardian Angel will defend us with confident enthusiasm. If we persevere in grace! If not, God forbid, then woe to us. As Saint Francis Xavier once said when advised to slow down in his "golden years" (I paraphrase), "What? Slow down? Does the captain of the ship pull in the oars when land is sighted? No, he rows the harder seeing his journey coming to an end."

Who will win the battle for your soul? Will your Guardian Angel prevail? Or will Old Scratch, basking in his arrogant bravado, be victorious because of the damning evidence that you so carelessly provided for him? Imagine that this is taking place right now. Think about the intense anxiety you would be experiencing. Imagine the final verdict, delivered by Our Lord, Whom you treated so presumptuously. The time to think about this is now, while you still have life on earth and time to expiate your sins by penance. Do it now—before you are tempted by envy, anger, and despair, and lured away by the false promises of the Father of Lies.

Thinking about the preceding is not particularly uplifting. Who wants to reflect on the particular judgment when you have been told that the "golden years" are the time in which you are supposed to be carefree, enjoying the fruits of your labor. But reflect on this you must. The salvation of your soul depends on it.

Lastly, if you are a serious Catholic, there will be no compromises in following the teachings of your Faith. You will recall that Christ clearly made this point in the Gospel of Saint Matthew, chapter 12, verse 30, when He stated, "He that is not with Me is against Me." As emphasized previously, Our Lord abhorred neutrality, particularly those lukewarm Catholics He equated as being vomit that He spewed from His mouth. This is a powerfully graphic image of how Our Lord felt about those who try "to sit on the fence" or "play both ends against the middle." Above all, don't let this characterization apply to you, especially in light of the fact that you are coming to the end of your life. You still have the opportunity to earn merit for the expiation of your sins and to lessen the temporal punishment for those of family and friends who are languishing in Purgatory. As a "Being Old" Catholic, you can serve as an example to the next generation on how to face life's adversities when your human powers are deteriorating and your demise may be just over the horizon.

Keep in mind the last line of Sonnet XVI, the poem written by John Milton on his blindness: "They also serve who only stand and wait." This may be what Our Lord expects of us — to carry our "Being Old" cross silently and patiently, without commotion and fanfare, but with the dignity and grace He intended.

Open Letters to Catholic Graduates is unique in its emphasis on the transition between college and the secular world, an emphasis sorely needed for the young Catholic today. Graduates are confronted with the task of facing the world and making something of themselves. This task is simultaneously exciting and perilous.

Graduates today will certainly feel the strong pull of the secular world and its allurements, but Dr. Lavin reminds them to not lose focus. *Open Letters to Catholic Graduates* exhorts graduates from high school and college to reaffirm their essential mission in life: to get to heaven. In his Open Letters, Lavin writes on topics of taking salvation seriously, forming true friendships, the dangers of capital sins, using psychology as a helpful aid, one's final end, and more.

Available at rafkapress.com

About the author

Paul Lavin received his Ph.D. in 1971. He is a clinical psychologist and the author of *Parenting the Overactive Child*. Lavin lives in Massachusetts and exclusively attends the traditional Latin Mass.

Dr. Lavin also wrote the following books on the Catholic Faith:

The Iron Man of China is about his uncle, Father Joseph Lavin, who served as a Maryknoll priest for twenty years before his expulsion from China by the Communists.

Keeping the Faith: A Young Catholic's Guide to Coping with a Secular World is for Catholic youth who will soon enter secular society.

Diabolical Satire: Satan's Response to the Conciliar Church is a witty, satirical look at the revolutionary changes in the Catholic Church since Vatican II.

Open Letter to Catholic Graduates exhorts graduates from high school and college to reaffirm their essential mission in life: to get to heaven.

Rafka Press
Uplifting Families —
One Book at a Time

Visit our website for more Catholic literature
www.rafkapress.com

www.ingramcontent.com/pod-product-compliance
Lightning Source LLC
Chambersburg PA
CBHW022116040426
42450CB00006B/723